# INFOPRENEURS

## Turning Data into Dollars

## H. Skip Weitzen

with

William "Biff" Genda

**John Wiley & Sons, Inc.**
New York • Chichester • Brisbane • Toronto • Singapore

Publisher: Stephen Kippur
Editor: David Sobel
Managing Editor: Ruth Greif
Editing, Design, and Production: Publications Development Company

Weitzen, H. Skip.
    Infopreneurs : turning data into dollars / by H. Skip Weitzen.
        p.    cm.
    ISBN 0-471-63371-2
    1. Data base industry—United States.    2. Information technology—United States.    I. Title.
HD9696.D363U68    1987                    87-28578
004'.068—dc19                              CIP

Printed in the United States of America

    10 9 8 7 6

This book is dedicated to my wife, Julia.

## TRADEMARKS AND COPYRIGHTS

# CONTENTS

# FOREWORD

Thousands of speeches have been made about it. Hundreds of articles have been written about it. There is really no shortage of books on it either. But the fascination with the application of information technologies will clearly continue from this century to the next. Why? Because each day we get the opportunity to witness yet another astonishing development in the use of one of man's greatest achievements—the computer. But what fascinates business people in these speeches, articles and books? The ingenious ways in which people apply the technology and subsequently create markets, industries, jobs, and most of all—money.

How many times have you said, "Why didn't I think of that?" or "I wonder how someone comes up with an idea like that?" or "How could I get in on this action?" I think *Infopreneurs* will be the answer for many people.

Along with Skip's first book *Telephone Magic, Infopreneurs* provides a primer for people who want to take advantage of today's information movement and management technologies. It is a down-to-earth, logical, plain language approach with a steady stream of examples that is sure to evoke the creative juices of any reader.

Perhaps the most worthwhile aspect of the book is the segmentation of these money-making ideas into clear categories to order your thinking. Each category outlines how infopreneurs are "doing more for less" from the leveraging and customizing of data base information to the easier access to it on a 24-hour basis. Many of the ideas revolve around the maximization of the computer, the telephone, and the credit card.

This "Information Triangle" is at the heart of most innovative ventures in business today. As such, the person who is able to master the integration of these elements is often tomorrow's new business sensation.

You might say that my personal and professional relationship with the author is symptomatic of our times. Skip and I have spent countless hours together sharing our joint fascination with this subject. We have acted as catalysts for each other's creativity. We have compared notes on the proven, as well as the latest in new applications and ventures—telemarketing, electronic order exchange, promotion management, teleconferencing, crisis management, voice and data networking innovations and opportunities. We have done this for over four years but have never met each other face to face.

*Infopreneurs* is more than a collection of success stories or a cookbook for would-be innovators, it is a catalyst for action. Whether you are a student, own your own business, or work for a large corporation, you cannot help but be influenced by this book. I have spent most of my 13 years with AT&T investigating, developing, and marketing new applications of information movement and management technologies. In that time, I have been fortunate to be associated with scores of talented scientists, engineers, marketers, clients, and individual innovators. *Infopreneurs* and *Telephone Magic* have made it easy for anyone to share in and play a role in this subject. I hope you will enjoy this book and be provoked into unleashing your creative applications' juices. Perhaps in Skip's next book, you and your ideas will be featured.

Happy Infopreneuring!

Peter R. de Tagyos
AT&T

# PREFACE

One evening while scribbling on a legal pad, I wrote out the words *information entrepreneur*. Continuing to write, I quickly glanced back at the two words. What happened next has no logical explanation. The two words combined to become one—*infopreneur*. I scrawled the word as I saw it and a week later visited the Office of Patents and Trademarks in Washington, D.C. On August 6, 1985, the commissioner registered the word "infopreneur," to describe information entrepreneurs, the new breed of entrepreneur ushering in the Information Age.

Int. Cl.: 16

Prior U.S. Cl.: 38

**United States Patent and Trademark Office**    Reg. No. 1,352,733   Registered Aug. 6, 1985

**TRADEMARK**
**PRINCIPAL REGISTER**

WEITZEN, HAROLD F. (UNITED STATES CIT-IZEN), DBA FORESIGHT AND PLANNING ANNAPOLIS, MD    FIRST USE 1-31-1984; IN COMMERCE 1-31-1984.

*Infopreneurs* is the story of new wine poured into old wineskins—a new breed of entrepreneur entering America's traditional business enterprises. History shows us that when new wine is poured into old wineskins, the wineskins burst. A century ago, industrialists were the new wine poured into the old wineskin of agrarian society. A revolution took place over who would rule the social and economic sectors of the Industrial Age—

farmers or industrialists.

By the close of the twentieth century, one key issue will have been settled as the new wine (infopreneurs) is poured into the old wineskins of industrial society: Who will dominate the social and economic sectors of the Information Age—

industrialists or infopreneurs.

## ACKNOWLEDGMENTS

*Infopreneurs* came about as the result of a good idea and extensive research, but most importantly, the encouragement and support of my family and friends. It is only appropriate that they be acknowledged for their part in this project.

Special thanks to my best friend and partner in life, Julia, whose love, acceptance, and forgiveness through our years together helped make this dream come true. Thanks for helping me grow.

My three daughters also deserve my deep-felt thanks: Jessica Grace, Cassandra Renee, and Tiffany Joy. I just hope I can be as accepting of your pursuits as you have been of mine.

I would like to acknowledge the fact that all creativity comes from one source. I am convinced that one night back in 1983 it was God's Holy Spirit that first placed into my mind the vision for *Infopreneurs*.

I would also like to remember the late Jonathan Coe, to whom I dedicated my first book. It was through his death from leukemia at age 29 that I came to realize just how unimportant all of my writings are compared with knowing God.

Thanks to my editor at John Wiley and Sons, David Sobel. He believed in the idea and had the wisdom to mold *Infopreneurs* into the quality product that it is today. Special thanks to my publisher, Stephen Kippur, managing editor Ruth Greif, and production editor, Nancy Marcus Land. Thank you also to Martha Jewett, senior editor at McGraw-Hill, who gave me my start as an author, and to Barbara Toniolo, one of the best teachers I have ever had.

Thank you to the faculty and staff at Anne Arundel Community College for their friendship and support over the years— David W. Hearne, George Stook, Ed Hiller, Bob Pollero, Dave Wiley, Anthony Pappas, Chief Information Officer Bill Reem, Guy Fish, Gary Thomas, Drema Marks, Katheryn Pfeiffer, Kathleen Ditmore, and of course, Karen Parks.

The following friends played a very special role during the incubation stage of this project. They breathed hope into the book when the words were first being placed on the page: Ron and Robin Zabiegalski, H. Preston and Joan Knepp, Gary Medovich, and Anita Schmied.

I would also like to acknowledge my brothers, Steve and Larry, who have challenged me over the years to never forget my roots.

Special thanks to environmental scanner, David Jamison, for providing much of the raw data for this book. Your friendship and feedback over the years are truly appreciated. Thanks to Carl Herrman for his artistic interpretation of the word, Infopreneur.

Special thanks to Gary Coleman and Michael Siegel, deans at the University of Maryland University College, for giving place to the first university-level course in America that focuses on information entrepreneurship.

In order to communicate these ideas I needed the help of a talented infopreneur. Sheryl Sieracki reviewed the first draft of this manuscript constantly asking, "Is this what you really want to say?" Thank you, Sheryl, for your dedication to this project.

Thanks again to my weekly prayer warriors and special family members who have encouraged me in my writings for the past several years: Jay Mitchell, Mike Moriarty, Tom Meekins, Eric Coolbaugh, Mike Peters, John Burris, Jim Banello, Vic and Cindy Primeaux, Barb and Ken Overman, Brad and Melinda Bettencourt, John and Kevin Odean, Pierre and Sandra Tullier, Brenda Chilcoat, Michelle Brandes, Barb Genda, Alan and Pauly Heller, Clare and Jack Morra, Tom and Virginia Whitelock, Wes and Ella Marie Harty, Fred and Arlene Weitzen.

## ABOUT THE AUTHOR

H. Skip Weitzen is president of the Annapolis, Maryland consulting firm, Foresight and Planning. As an information marketing consultant Mr. Weitzen has worked with, consulted for, and written about hundreds of infopreneurs and corporations participating in the current Information Revolution. He is an adjunct professor of Management Studies at The University of Maryland University College where he teaches the first university-level course in America dedicated to information entrepreneurship. His first book, *Telephone Magic: How to Tap the Phone's Marketing Potential in Your Business* (McGraw-Hill), was selected as one of the top 30 business books of 1987 by Soundview Executive Book Summaries.

## SPECIAL ACKNOWLEDGMENT

William "Biff" Genda served as technical editor for *Infopreneurs*. He spent the past year thinking with me to shape many of these new ideas. His technical background and knowledge of the information marketplace helped crystallize concepts which began as vague thoughts. Mr. Genda is an engineer with the ARINC Research Corporation in Annapolis, Maryland and director of JobMate®, an international placement service for the information industry.

# PART ONE

# TURNING DATA INTO DOLLARS

**INFOPRENEUR**

A new word about a new breed of entrepreneur

in-fō-prə-nûr′

A person who gathers, organizes, and disseminates information as a business venture or as a value-added service.

# KEY TO INFOPRENEURSHIP: DO MORE FOR LESS

The buying and selling of information accounts for more than $16.4 billion in today's marketplace. Infopreneurs who succeed in turning data into dollars during the Information Revolution will do so by honoring history's timeless principles and lessons. One such principle, "doing more for less," links all forms of progress, regardless of economic sector. Even in their most rudimentary activities, infopreneurs strive to "do more for less." The fact that the Information Revolution was sparked by infopreneurs doing more work at less cost, using fewer resources, to provide a better service seems to validate this bottom-line principle.

## The Information Marketplace

| Economic Sector | Industry Sales in Millions ($) | Information Sales in Millions ($) |
|---|---|---|
| Consumer goods | $ 846,995 | $ 4,090 |
| Consumer services | 110,604 | 1,440 |
| Construction | 72,351 | 425 |
| Industrial goods | 1,567,317 | 2,190 |
| Agriculture | NA | 230 |
| Distribution services | 733,429 | 2,915 |
| Intermediate/professional services | 429,337 | 4,420 |
| Government/nonprofit | NA | 715 |
| | $3,823,033 | $16,425 |

*Notes:* Industry sales figures derived from the proprietary sorting of the Fortune 500 Industrials, 500 Services, and a sample of 123 foreign companies by Hambrecht and Quist Incorporated.

Information sales figures are institutional research estimates prepared by Hambrecht and Quist Incorporated, 1987.

# DOING MORE FOR LESS

Doing more for less is evident within each of America's major economic sectors: farming, manufacturing, and services. Turning the clock back to 1776 when America was founded, four million farms employed 90 percent of the workforce. A single farmer could then feed three people. Two centuries later, technological, social, and economic advances brought a revolution to the agrarian sector of the American economy:

- The number of farms was reduced by more than 40 percent to 2.3 million,
- Employment in the agrarian sector dropped from 90 percent down to just 3 percent of the work force,
- One farmer could feed 77 people, a significant jump in farm productivity.

4

Today America has fewer farmers working on fewer farms using fewer resources to feed more people. In other words, farmers are "doing more for less."

America's second major economic sector, manufacturing, is currently undergoing its own revolution. During the past 40 years, three events changed manufacturing forever:

- Computers created large-scale information management possibilities.
- Sputnik created satellite communications.
- OPEC created an oil embargo.

The oil price shocks of the 1970s caused a 1200 percent increase in the cost of a barrel of oil, slowed manufacturing productivity, and shattered the foundation of America's industrial economy.

Manufacturers soon took advantage of low energy prices and low labor costs by relocating to foreign nations. Computers and satellite communications from the United States now control production and inventories overseas. As goods production moves overseas and the American service sector expands, more than half the jobs in the United States have become information-based. An economic reorganization is underway as smokestack industries give way to information-based firms.

The shrinking manufacturing sector of the U.S. economy should be viewed as an attempt to "do more for less." If automated manufacturing and global wage leveling continue, the U.S. manufacturing sector will probably decline from 23 percent of the workforce today, to less than 5 percent within the next 20 years—all because progress does "more for less."

The third major economic sector in America, services, already comprises 74 percent of the labor force. At the heart of the service economy are infopreneurs who account for 40 percent of its economic activity. The rapid growth of information activity within the service sector was stimulated by advances in the computer industry—perhaps the best model of "doing more for less." For example:

5

- In 1955 computerized information was processed on 200 BPI tape density in just over an hour at a cost of $14.54.
- Just 30 years later, computers processed the same information on 38,000 BPI tape density in one second for less than a dime!

Today more computers generate more information at less cost and in less time using fewer resources than ever before. In other words, computers help infopreneurs "do more for less."

The Industrial Age produced significant advances hindered by the economic impact of toxic pollutants, a national economy that fluctuates with shortages and gluts in oil supplies, and the introduction of cheaper and more durable products by foreign nations. American business has turned to information for solutions to these problems since sufficient information helps reduce the margin of error in the decision-making process.

When you reconsider your future as an infopreneur, apply the time-proven principle of "doing more for less." The basic strategies that help infopreneurs do more for less can be summed up in three words that rhyme:

CONSOLIDATE, ISOLATE, and POTENTIATE.

To do more for less, infopreneurs need to *consolidate* information which eliminates computers, reduces overhead, and brings about a more effective utilization of resources.

Progress today, marked by the ever-present need to do more for less, requires infopreneurs to *isolate* the top 20 percent of their constituents which generate 80 percent of the revenue. An infopreneur can then invest the first marketing dollar where it will have its greatest impact and bring the best return.

To *potentiate*, or achieve information's full value, infopreneurs need to improve productivity while simultaneously reducing costs.

Each of these three strategies is evident within the seven ways infopreneurs turn data into dollars. These key thoughts will reoccur and be expanded on in chapters that follow.

# LEVERAGE DATA BASE INFORMATION

Data bases are comprehensive collections of interrelated information that allow manipulation and retrieval of this stored information to service a wide variety of applications. The data can range from names and addresses to recipes and lists to inventories and bid specifications. This computerized library of up-to-date information represents a vital asset in today's competitive environment.

- *Consolidate.* The basic feature of a data base is that information can be stored, updated, sorted, and retrieved in a variety of ways. As a result, infopreneurs can link disparate bits of information, eliminating much of the time-consuming, labor-intensive activities of data entry to create new files. The consolidation of data combined with the computer's sort function allows infopreneurs to generate new data and to look at old data in new ways.
- *Isolate.* Data bases can be leveraged to isolate customer needs and desires. Selective access of a file, known as segmentation, allows for targeted, personalized communications with key constituents and avoids such elaborate communications with fringe audiences.
- *Potentiate.* Infopreneurs who leverage data base information experience its full value when the same information accessed by Fortune 500 companies becomes available to solve their problems, or when the infopreneur can derive new insights from established historical data, or when the data base sort function correlates seemingly unrelated data to provide the infopreneur with new perspectives not previously available, or when new products and services can be designed from data base characteristics.

Infopreneurs do more for less with their data bases as they collect, store, and sort the vital information about their constituents. Infopreneurs then leverage their data bases to discover new ways to turn data into dollars.

7

## CUSTOMIZE INFORMATION

Infopreneurs need not be experts to customize information. Once they understand the problem before them, they simply need to know where to get the data, how to sort through the data, and how to present the data to decision makers.

- *Consolidate.* To consolidate information, infopreneurs must be cognizant of all sources of information such as data bases, government source documents, printed materials, television and radio, advertisements and promotions, seminars and workshops, libraries, and organizational knowledge or experience. Infopreneurs then collect, store, and consolidate the needed information using electronic storage systems such as computer tapes and disks, microform, videotapes, and optical disks.
- *Isolate.* Infopreneurs help separate irrelevant information (that which will not be useful in making decisions) from relevant information (that which is vital in making well-informed decisions). Useful information must be isolated, then systematically arranged and presented to improve decision making.
- *Potentiate.* Customized information is potentiated when it provides its answers in a form that is easily understood. One example is computer-generated data converted into color graphics which helps people absorb three times more information than before, and in less time.

Infopreneurs must regard information as a resource equal in value to capital, personnel, and facilities because it costs money to acquire, process, store, distribute, and protect. Only when information achieves that status can infopreneurs do more for less through customized information and turn data into dollars.

## FACILITATE ACCESS TO INFORMATION

The Information Revolution is highlighted by the proliferation of scientific articles: In 1986, up to 10,000 articles were written each day. By 1990, the number of articles will total 20,000 a day. Infopreneurs facilitate access to information by sorting through massive quantities of data, random facts, and isolated communications.

- *Consolidate.* Infopreneurs consolidate information using technology which electronically accesses, files, stores, sorts, retrieves, and distributes information.
- *Isolate.* Infopreneurs have isolated the types of most frequently obtained information requested through on-line services: credit and finance (39%); securities and commodities (35%); legal, medical, and professional (13%); scientific and technical (6%); abstract, bibliography, and text (5%); and nonbusiness consumer information (2%).
- *Potentiate.* An Industrial Age paradigm states that knowledge is power. Today knowledge is not power, rather knowledge *about* knowledge is power. In the Information Age, knowing how to find information, knowing how to present information, and knowing how the information will be used is just as important as knowing what the information is about. Knowing "how" is the secret to potentiating information.

Consider that the amount of information available today is likely to double within the next four years. Infopreneurs must know what information is needed, how to find this information, and how to present the information in a form that improves communications, decision making, or action, in order to do more for less and turn data into dollars.

## SPEED UP THE FLOW OF INFORMATION

In today's business context, the velocity of information increases through technologies and techniques, which are as different in nature and function as the left hemisphere of the brain is from the right. Technologies used today to speed up the flow of information include computers, telephones, satellites, videodisks, and televisions. Techniques that provide insights into the early signs of economic, political, and social change include content analysis, environmental scanning, and inferential reading.

- *Consolidate.* Infopreneurs who consolidate information are faced with a new challenge: How to quickly sort through vast quantities of information in less time using fewer resources to provide greater value in the marketplace.
- *Isolate.* Infopreneurs speed up the flow of information to isolate new options from the gathered, stored, retrieved, and transferred information. This strategy improves productivity, reduces costs, and provides a competitive edge.
- *Potentiate.* To potentiate information, infopreneurs require systems which can instantly generate reports, manipulate data, analyze "what if" scenarios, and provide access to data. Potentiated information is the most efficient and cost-effective use of information available.

Infopreneurs who can instantly generate, send, and receive information or identify trends and early signs of change will do more for less and turn data into dollars.

## REPACKAGE INFORMATION

Infopreneurs repackage information by organizing it, then recombining it to bring about new information products and services. The process starts with a search for a unique opportunity which may lie dormant because no one has recognized its potential.

- *Consolidate.* Infopreneurs consolidate information to uncover previously unrelated but potentially relatable opportunities. Success results when a simple, yet focused, solution is applied to previously unmet or unperceived needs.

- *Isolate.* Infopreneurs isolate solutions to unmet needs from among the five forms of information: voice, data, text, images, and pictures.
- *Potentiate.* Repackaged information is potentiated when it is integrated into new products to improve the rate of success and increase profits.

Infopreneurs *think small* to find a niche, *do it right* to get a toehold in the market, *make a profit* with their information, then *expand* their applications. They require broad goals, specific objectives, and flexible strategies as a framework to repackage information, do more for less, and turn data into dollars.

## PROVIDE AROUND-THE-CLOCK DELIVERY OF INFORMATION

During today's Information Revolution, information technology processes and delivers information around the clock. Infopreneurs who offer information 24 hours a day can reshape the way products and services meet the changing needs in the marketplace.

- *Consolidate.* Information has been consolidated to the point that a person can dial a single phone number through a Touch Tone phone from anywhere in the world and receive information about any product or service at any hour.
- *Isolate.* Around-the-clock delivery of information helps isolate new markets and customers. Businesses using 24-hour toll-free phone numbers receive 25 percent of their calls between 6 P.M. and 9 P.M.—after traditional working hours are completed.
- *Potentiate.* Around-the-clock delivery of information is potentiated when it can simultaneously capture new customer information, reduce overhead expenses, and create new marketing opportunities.

11

By the end of the century, infopreneurs will deliver society's information 24 hours a day to do more for less and turn data into dollars.

## INTEGRATE THE INFORMATION TRIANGLE

One of the most important dynamics to the success of infopreneurs is the *Information Triangle*, which integrates the computer/telephone/electronic funds transfer technologies to provide immediate payment for information generated and delivered.

- *Consolidate*. The Information Triangle consolidates corporate resources to improve information productivity and eliminate costly intermediaries.
- *Isolate*. Infopreneurs integrate the Information Triangle to isolate methods of generating immediate payment for the information they provide.
- *Potentiate*. As information technology centralizes specialized services and decentralizes routine interactions, infopreneurs integrate the Information Triangle to potentiate information which rearranges the methods by which goods, services, and information are delivered worldwide.

The Information Triangle offers business its next productivity breakthrough. As infopreneurs integrate the Information Triangle into traditional business functions, they can do more for less, increase the value of information, and *instantly* turn data into dollars.

## YOUR SECRET TO SUCCESS: DO MORE FOR LESS

Progress in the marketplace is always measured by how well you accomplish one thing: Provide *better* and *better* information to *more* and *more* people at *lower* and *lower* costs. In

12

other words, the infopreneurs' secret to success is measured by how well they "do more for less."

Following World War II, the American economy was strong and the market placed new demands for goods and services. Thus it was easy for corporations to succeed. Within a few years, the rumblings of the Information Revolution shattered the industrial economic model; business forecasts and learning curves lost their meanings. Today companies can rarely afford to make a major mistake and still hope to compete in the world economy.

The Information Revolution brings a new impetus to America's economic model. In the Agrarian Age, manpower was the impetus. Human labor was the energy that cleared the land, planted the crops, and fed the nation. In the Industrial Age, inexpensive energy was the impetus. It fueled blast furnaces, transported people, and heated homes. As we enter the Information Age, information is becoming the impetus. Information, not manpower or energy, now launches new industries.

History shows that the agrarian, manufacturing, and service sectors are not exempt from the timeless value of "doing more for less." Why should anyone think that infopreneurs of the information sector will be? As you contemplate strategies for the remainder of the Information Revolution, never lose sight of the three steps that will help you do more for less:

## CONSOLIDATE—ISOLATE—POTENTIATE

Since the information industry brings with it its own economy, infopreneurs can bypass traditional economic structures as they shape the new economic order. Because infopreneurs do not manufacture products or transport goods, financial institutions play a smaller role in the growth of these new ventures. Infopreneurs, an economic and sociological phenomenon, have emerged as new leaders in a new economic environment.

As we enter the Information Age, infopreneurs are establishing a new set of business standards. For example, when in history could a 13-year-old eighth grade student become an energy consultant to corporations such as J.C. Penney and General Mills? Or when was it ever possible for a college dropout to build a Fortune 500 company before he reached the age of 30? Or when could a woman earn $240,000 a year just by selling information from her home?

Since only 5 percent of the population benefits directly and significantly from the upheaval that accompanies revolutionary changes, conduct your own personal inventory of what it will take to become part of this fortunate 5 percent. As we complete the shift into the Information Age, successful infopreneurs will turn data into dollars and information into income as they honor the time-proven principle of history by doing more for less.

Will you be one of them?

# LEVERAGE DATA BASE INFORMATION

Just as investors leverage assets to increase their net worth, infopreneurs leverage data bases and information data banks to create new business opportunities. The ability to manipulate a data base is as significant as the computer itself: On-line data base services have become the foundation of information operations and the brains behind the Information Revolution.

As stated earlier, a data base is a comprehensive collection of interrelated data that allows data manipulation and retrieval in order to service a wide variety of applications. The data can range widely—from names and addresses to recipes and lists to inventories and bid specifications. One vital asset

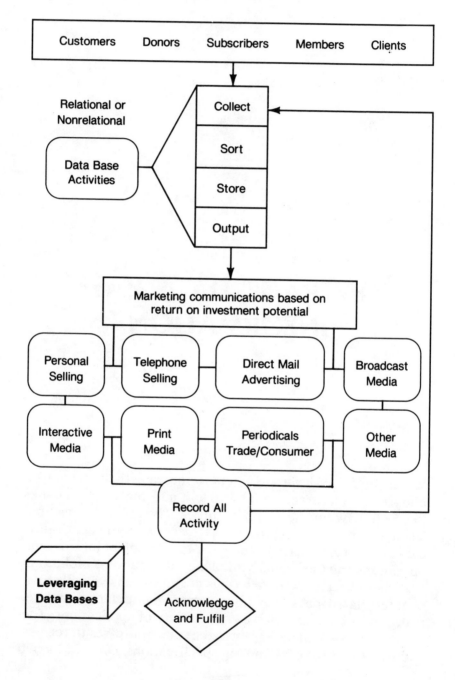

Customers    Donors    Subscribers    Members    Clients

Relational or
Nonrelational

Data Base
Activities

Collect
Sort
Store
Output

Marketing communications based on
return on investment potential

Personal
Selling

Telephone
Selling

Direct Mail
Advertising

Broadcast
Media

Interactive
Media

Print
Media

Periodicals
Trade/Consumer

Other
Media

Record All
Activity

Leveraging
Data Bases

Acknowledge
and Fulfill

16

in today's competitive environment is this computerized library of up-to-date information.

Creating and managing a data base requires a different way of thinking about business. Rather than a product or service being the most basic unit of business, a customer data base plays that role. It creates a new set of management, marketing, and measurement opportunities by combining the files and records of a company's customers.

Information entered *once* on a data base can be stored, updated, sorted, and retrieved in a variety of ways. As a result, infopreneurs can link disparate bits of information eliminating much of the time-consuming, labor-intensive activities of data entry to create new files. The analytical capability of the sorting function allows infopreneurs to create new data and look at old data in new ways.

In 1987, nearly 500 on-line services offered more than 3000 data bases; a decade earlier there were none. The major factors affecting the emergence and subsequent growth of data bases include:

- *Time and storage advances.* Faster execution and increased storage facilitates access to processed information. Technical breakthroughs have placed the power of mainframe computers in the hands of infopreneurs.
- *Cost reductions.* Technological advances have reduced computing costs. For just one dollar, an infopreneur can execute 100 million computer instructions or buy on-line storage of 50,000 characters for one year.
- *Advances in system architecture.* New time-share architecture systems provide on-line interaction rather than the delayed access of batch processing. The new system designs increase an infopreneur's productivity by allowing easier real-time manipulation of accessed data.

Data bases are the latest phase in the evolution of the computer. Network link-ups to computer data bases help infopreneurs not only obtain general market information and support data for research, but also create marketing plans, pricing strategies, distribution channels, advertising programs, and financing opportunities. Infopreneurs can search for information through three types of on-line data bases:

- *Reference data bases* provide information on topics found in books and articles.
- *Full-text data bases* call up the complete text of stories and articles on the computer screen.
- *Source data bases* provide data such as stock quotes and company information.

A fourth type of data base is emerging. *Interactive data bases* are being used to supplement existing data bases as users enter and retrieve data. Although the quality and accuracy of inputs are sometimes questioned, infopreneurs find this type of real-time information critical to their real-time decisions.

When infopreneurs create data bases, they generally approach the task in two distinct phases. In the first phase—front-end activities, the infopreneur plans the data base and management reports, then enters the data. In the second phase—back-end activities, the infopreneur sorts and retrieves the data. How well the back-end activities function depends on the design and accuracy of the front-end effort.

Infopreneurs who leverage data base information accrue several benefits:

- The same information accessed by Fortune 500 companies becomes available to solve the problems of the info-preneur.
- The infopreneur can derive new insights from established trends of historical data.
- The data base sort function correlates seemingly unrelated data to provide the infopreneur with new perspectives not previously available.
- When aimed at actual customers, an infopreneur's data base marketing and management program can cost less per dollar of sale than any other media strategy.
- An accurate picture of a customer's value to an info-preneur can be established through a number of controlled variables.

- New products and services that target existing customers can be designed from data base characteristics.
- Infopreneurs can add data obtained through research to customer records.

These benefits have given the Information Revolution many success stories of infopreneurs who have created and leveraged information data bases.

## DATA BASE MANAGER

In 1969, John Groman and three other Harvard Business School graduates founded Epsilon Data Management, Inc. They raised $100,000 on the basis of what venture capitalists considered a valuable concept: Fusing computer technology with sophisticated marketing techniques to reach relatively large numbers of people cost-efficiently.

Epsilon was first established under the name Fraternal Systems. It assisted fraternal organizations by computerizing their membership lists. The firm's first client was Sigma Alpha Epsilon; nine other fraternities signed on as clients in the first year. Fraternal Systems soon built data base management systems for nonfraternity, nonprofit organizations, including the Boston Symphony Orchestra. Once fraternities were no longer its only clients, the firm's name was changed to Epsilon Data Management.

Epsilon's marketing strategy was to obtain one client in each particular area of the nonprofit industry, such as a hospital or cultural organization, then establish a reputation for fundraising within that area. The company soon added commercial clients to its roster to account for half of its revenues. Today Epsilon provides data base management services to more than 250 commercial and nonprofit companies nationwide.

It was Groman's computer knowledge and marketing expertise that led to the company's growth from a five-man office to a national corporation with 700 employees and $50 million in annual sales. Along the way Groman pioneered the multibillion-dollar direct response marketing industry. Groman's data base marketing programs employ computer marketing information systems to identify and personally communicate with his customers' most profitable file segments.

Although Groman has developed marketing programs for hundreds of organizations, his most noteworthy accomplishment has come from integrating creative concepts with computer technology. In particular, he led the movement that merged sophisticated market data bases with direct marketing strategies through advanced segmentation techniques. The results led to enhanced market responsiveness through the isolation of three key ingredients: measurability, selectivity, and immediate response.

- *Measurability.* The results of each marketing effort can be quantified, making comparisons among the marketing strategies to develop a profit ranking. Refined marketing strategies are based on analysis of the most profitable returns. Communication response is measured through devices such as:
  - An address or toll-free number in broadcast ads.
  - A coupon with a toll-free number in print ads.
  - A bound-in reply card or envelope in publications.
  - A bounce-back device in receipts, shipping invoices, or premium and product deliveries.
- *Selectivity.* Computer sorting pinpoints segments of a file that produce the best return on investment and preselects advertising audiences. Without this capability, marketers cannot differentiate one viewer from another or one reader from another.
- *Immediate response.* Failure to design an immediate response into the message is the single most common mistake made in direct response marketing. Immediate response can best be generated through the use of issues that make a strong emotional impact, imply overwhelming benefits, or challenge the audience.

Derived from the client's data base, these elements help create direct marketing programs with the flexibility to sell products and services for commercial clients or raise funds for non-profit clients. Groman's use of these ingredients leads to enhanced market responsiveness in nearly any situation.

Epsilon was originally begun to integrate information technology to create data bases for clients. John Groman eventually leveraged the information from these data bases to build one of the largest data base marketing companies in the world.


## LAWSUIT DATA BASE

One night, Detroit attorney Paul Huth, then age 28, was discussing with his wife who is an anesthetist and his father-in-law who is a physician the problem of the increasing number of suits being filed. The physician declared that most plaintiffs were at one time plaintiffs in other litigations. A bet was made: Huth wagered that he could isolate the potential plaintiffs among his father-in-law's patients and show that this is not the case. Huth started by obtaining from an insurance company a list of people who had filed malpractice lawsuits. He visited the local courthouse and obtained the names of people who had filed lawsuits in his father-in-law's district. He cross-referenced those names with the ones from the insurance company. Huth lost the bet. More than one-third of those who had brought forth a suit had been a plaintiff at some time in the past.

Huth concluded that it might be useful to know the litigation background of potential new patients. He then started Physician's Alert, a national information service that isolates suit filers within a physician's practice.

Physician's Alert was formed at a time when Detroit's malpractice litigation was reaching crisis proportions. Huth hired researchers to work at county courthouses. Subscribing physicians call a researcher on a beeper and provide the name of the prospective patient. The researcher compares the name to the information in the public dominion data base at the courthouse and alerts the doctor whether or not the patient had filed a lawsuit.

To expand his business, Huth ran a small ad in the local newspaper. A Detroit newspaper reporter read the ad and wrote a story about Physician's Alert. The AP and UPI wires picked it up and the story ran in nearly every newspaper across the country.

Huth was featured in *Newsweek* and *Inc.* and appeared on the *Today* show. He received 80 requests for franchises from 26 states. Companies called wanting to buy him out or create a publicly owned corporation. In 1984, Huth joined with I.P. Sharp and Associates, which specializes in public domain data bases. Physician's Alert was then able to take advantage of Sharp's international networking capabilities.

Although Huth's idea was controversial, essentially all he did was make public information available at a reasonable price. Huth financed the project out-of-pocket. He bought equipment, rented space, and hired staff to work at courthouses. The service spread quickly by word-of-mouth through the corridors at the hospital. The doctors hired Huth as a way to avoid paying for meritless litigation. Physician's Alert helped them control some of the risk in their practices.

Huth knew that if he failed to expand fast enough, a bigger operation would come in and take over the market. He then hooked up with a company that had both the resources and technical capability to expand Physician's Alert rapidly.

Huth defines his niche as the marketing of public domain data bases at a cost the average person can afford. Huth actually created a market for the information. People were educated to the fact that they could gain some decision-making information by looking at those particular histories. Huth caught the attention of the market when he declared that many people who sue are repeat plaintiffs, and that information is readily available through Physician's Alert.

The success of Physician's Alert can be attributed to good timing. The service came at a crisis point in the medical malpractice industry. In addition, the natural controversy between physicians and lawyers caught the interest of media. Once the media heard about this unique venture, it helped create the market interest. The benefits of this media coverage is that its relative value would have cost Huth millions of dollars had he purchased it as paid advertising.

Today, customers call a toll-free number. A bank of operators tap into the data base to provide the information. The data base is compiled by various means—courthouse disks, printouts, or researchers gathering the information manually.

On a national level, American Medical Association statistics show a 100 percent increase in claims between 1976 and 1983. In the past, the nation's 420,000 physicians have expressed the need for a lawsuit prevention service and Physician's Alert provides it. The service has been successful in minimizing lawsuits and costly litigation, and reducing the number of out-of-court settlements.

With Physician's Alert, "professional" plaintiffs who routinely file suits now have a difficult time proceeding beyond a physician's waiting room. With the knowledge that a prior lawsuit has been filed, doctors have the option to refuse to take these people as patients, to charge them more for the additional risk, or to accept them (while exercising extreme caution).

Huth has created new markets for the same data base information under the names Landlord Alert, Lawyers Alert, Bankers Alert, and Insurance Alert.


## MUNICIPAL DATA BASE

In 1983, the Civic Information Techniques Exchange (Civitex) began as an offshoot of the nonprofit public interest group The National Municipal League. Infopreneur Ron Kim serves as the project manager over the data base, which contains abstracts on some 2,300 projects.

Civitex was formed to fill a need: To provide shared information on problems that exist among cities and communities. Civitex obtains information from cities and towns on a wide range of topics including low-income housing, food banks, and graffiti.

Rather than providing information from files or institutional memory, Ron Kim and his staff set up a system whereby citizens can obtain computerized data base information that will help them solve their community problems. Civitex charges a data base search fee of $10.

Civitex fills the niche of an information clearinghouse. It provides profiles or abstracts on the various projects of local communities. Since most projects are infinitely more complex than the 500-word abstract, the client is provided with a phone number of a contact person who can provide more detail. The contact is usually the person who originally donated the information. A new service recently introduced is a newsletter that links all the users of Civitex—some 8000 individuals and institutions.

Some of the most often requested areas of information include homelessness, drug abuse, teenage pregnancies, youth programs, beautification projects, economic growth, and child abuse.

The marketing plan Civitex implemented to get started included mass mailings to prospective users and advertisements in specialty magazines subscribed to by targeted constituents.

Citizen participation is what makes Civitex unique. Users of the data base fall into three basic categories: citizens, local government officials, and people involved in nonprofit groups such as United Way or daycare foundations. Civitex operators listen to a caller's problem, search the data base for similar subjects, and forward, by mail, one-page abstracts.

Once Civitex developed a network of citizens with a common basis of interest (improving their cities), the service took off. Today Civitex answers 80 to 100 queries a month with information from its data base.

## DATA BASE OF EXPERTS

R. Donald Gamache, co-founder of Innotech Corporation (Trumbull, CT), leverages his data base of experts and information to differentiate between good ideas and quality ideas.

The end result is the introduction of new product ideas for his clients.

Innotech is retained by some of America's largest corporations to create product and service ideas. The company receives $15–22,000 a month per client, dependent on whether a royalty on the new product's gross sales can be negotiated.

In today's competitive marketplace, "good" ideas are not good enough. Gamache has spent years learning how to generate "quality" ideas, ones that fit directly into a client's product mix.

Once retained by a client, Innotech starts by conducting a one-day data-gathering session at the client's office. The client is represented by a product management team of about a half-dozen people from various departments throughout the company. The purpose of the meeting is to determine the type of product the company wants to introduce, and the company's criteria for making the product successful.

Next, Innotech sorts through its computer data base of some 4000 experts, searching for authorities in that field. Program managers discuss the project with those specialists and invite them to participate.

Infopreneurs from Innotech then host expert sessions with the selected participants. Hundreds of ideas for new products are generated during a typical three-hour meeting, and information surfaces regarding economics and trends that may affect the product ideas.

The product ideas resulting from these sessions are presented to the client's product management team. The team then determines which ideas are worth pursuing. The program manager returns to the data base to search for a new set of specialists who can narrow the focus of the product ideas and help identify the appropriate markets. If needed, other meetings are held to redefine the ideas from the previous meetings or generate new product ideas.

As a result of this process, hundreds of ideas are narrowed down to one quality idea that is presented to the client decision maker. This idea usually does not represent a major innovation. Rather, it tends to fit easily into the client's product mix.

Innotech depends on the company's management team to carry the product idea through the corporate culture then launch the product. To be successful, the quality idea must overcome the "not invented here" syndrome within the corporation. So Innotech tries to locate a young executive who can champion the product idea through to completion.

The ability to create new ideas is merely part of what sets R. Donald Gamache apart as an infopreneur. His company's success can be related to its ability to leverage a data base of more than 4,000 experts to create "quality" ideas for its clients.

## DATA BASE OF SCOFFLAWS

Infopreneur Thomas Gleed knew what to do with a data base of "dead beats" when he found one: Turn the data into dollars. Gleed is the founder of Tele-Collection, Inc. which was formed to leverage the data base of scofflaws in local municipalities. Using voice-activated recordings and a computer, Gleed brings the voice of police authorities into the homes of motorists who ignore parking tickets or fail to buy vehicle stickers. In its second year of business, Tele-Collection collected $750,000.

The process starts with a municipality's providing a list of scofflaws to Tele-Collection. A warning letter is sent which is followed by a phone call through trained telephone "sales" representatives who ensure that the call is placed to the correct party. When the appropriate person comes on the line the recorded voice of a police officer is played saying that this call is official business and the answers will be recorded.

The voice of the police officer asks whether the person is aware of several unpaid parking tickets. If there is silence at the other end, the voice repeats the question. The voice then outlines the actions to be taken if the fine is not paid—lawsuit, warrant for arrest, or the use of a tire lock. The caller is often silent. The voice then states that no parking violation is worth that much trouble or embarrassment.

The call is then followed up by a personalized letter which gives the scofflaw an opportunity to mail in a check.

Tele-Collection provides city officials with an updated data base of names and addresses of those who have been contacted. Tele-Collection is then paid 40 percent of the monies collected by the city for parking ticket violations. Fees may vary based on the complexity of the communications program.

Tele-Collection is an offshoot of the parent company, Concensus, Inc., which provides direct response and telemarketing services for political and charitable fundraising purposes. Infopreneur Gleed sees the application of Tele-Collection to improve the collections effort on behalf of revenue-thin governments and businesses.

A data base of scofflaws has actually become a source of badly needed revenue. And what can generate revenue is worth pursuing. Tele-Collection is a case where leveraging a data base was the correct response to a fundamental change in business. With information storage requirements becoming so unwieldy, municipalities turned to the computer as a solution, while at the same time opening up a revenue-generating opportunity.

Infopreneurs like Thomas Gleed now combine the sophistication of data base management with modern marketing to respond to the changes in the environment. Just as many traditional marketing techniques often depended on intuition, today's information opportunities are being created by that same intuitive process.

Gleed takes his customer's data base and:

- segments the names to identify those with the greatest revenue potential,
- tests new ways to reach and motivate them to comply with the law,
- communicates with them in highly personal ways, and
- measures results to make adjustments to the approach.

The result is leveraging a data base and turning data into dollars.

# LEVERAGING DATA BASES

## Create Your Own Data Base

The data base can break business down into its functioning parts, which can be studied and improved. Quantitative descriptions can then provide insights into the potential of each new business opportunity.

Some of the best sources of information for a data base are areas where names can be easily accessed: Customer files, rosters of professional organizations, even the Yellow Pages. With negligible storage costs for information, data base management is no longer a technical problem to be solved, but an opportunity to be leveraged.

Electronic data base management allows the information generated to be quickly summarized. Because this information ultimately supports business decisions, accuracy of data entered is paramount. The data entered should be cross-checked.

The system design should include easy access to files, allowance for frequent updates, security, and, most importantly, be responsive to the user's needs. Client-friendly data bases are made up of files, which are composed of records, which are derived from fields. A data base could include the following elements, depending on the needs of the infopreneur:

1. Name Block including
   Individual or company name
   Salutation
   Title
2. Address Block including
   Street address
   City, state, and zip and country code
3. Customer Information including
   Operation of data
      Credited division          Sales contact
      Territory code             Priority code

Customer profile
    Industry classification    Phone number
    Names of contacts    Numbers of employees
    Sales volume

Demographic profile
    Citizenship    Occupation
    Date of birth    Sex
    Residence type    Education
    Marital status

Psychographic profile
    Product preference    Buying motivation
    Interest and lifestyle

4. Customer Interactions including

Inquiries and correspondence
    Date    Source code

Purchase information
    Date    Product type
    Sales amount    Source
    Promotion

Promotions
    Date    Source code

Responses
    Date    Type
    Source    Value

Fulfillment action
    Date    Materials sent

Research responses
    Date of responses    Coded answers

The ultimate goal is to place a data base into the context of the management system so that infopreneurs can solve complex problems and meet the needs of the marketplace. Once the information is entered, the infopreneur sorts and organizes the data to help plan management or marketing strategies. Computer data can be segmented to create personalized, targeted marketing programs. Through foresight and planning, the data base can then be used to fulfill customer requests.

## Use On-Line Data Bases

A 1987 industry estimate puts the number of daily electronic information service users at about 125,000. Sales of this electronic information will top $3.4 billion in 1988, with a registered growth rate of 23 percent per year. The majority of on-line research, however, is performed by relatively few information specialists.

To date, the Information Revolution has not reached its full potential because on-line data bases tend to be expensive and difficult to use. It is mostly infopreneurs within the corporate environment who can justify the cost for on-line services. The most effective uses of on-line data bases include:

- Downloading information into the computer in digital form, which allows it to be manipulated easily without having to be keyed in again.
- Loading statistics directly into spreadsheets, which makes for instant analysis.
- Screening data by the computer, which reduces the sheer volume of data and prevents information overload.

Many data base services are available. Some of the most popular include:

- *The Source* and *Compuserve*—Provide a full range of data base activities, ranging from electronic mail to stock quotes.
- *Dialog*—Contains more than 200 data bases but specializes in bibliographic services.
- *Newsnet*—Offers a full line of newsletters.
- *Nexis*—Provides a full-text data base of newspapers and magazines.
- *Predicast*—Provides abstracts of more than 1200 trade journals and corporate literature.
- *Dow Jones News/Retrieval Service*—Includes financial publications and transcripts from popular television programs.

To enter these electronic libraries the user needs a modem, a personal computer or terminal, communications software, and a telephone. The user dials a local telephone number to link up with computers at other sites. Access to a desired data base is made possible through special passwords. Charges for on-line data base services are on an hourly connect-time rate, plus communication costs via one of the public networks. To save time and money when working on-line, consider these eight principles:

1. Go on-line during nonpeak hours for faster and cheaper service.
2. Keep notes of your on-line search strategies.
3. Learn the *help* and *escape* sequences for the on-line service.
4. Use a thesaurus to reduce the number of missed references.
5. Minimize typing errors, which lead to erroneous searches.
6. Know where to find the needed on-line data.
7. Use specialized software to speed up the search.
8. Bypass the menus and prompts once you are familiar with a system.

Some of the most helpful on-line data base information is available in hard copy, including: *The Directory of On-Line Data Bases, The Directory of On-Line Professionals,* and a magazine called *The Microcomputer User's Guide to Information On-Line.*

## Data Bases Are Everywhere

Data bases are simply collections of raw information. By systematizing this information, new opportunities to build a data base are created.

For example, the publisher of *Equus* magazine was often questioned about horse training, transportation, health, and other issues important to horse owners. He compiled answers to more than 3000 questions and stored them in his computer.

Subscribers were invited to mail in questions which were keyed into the computer and answered overnight. The data base then was offered in the magazine's subscription promotions and billed as a "99-cent sale." Subscribers who accessed the data base (for just 99 cents above the subscription price) received a manual and printed forms on which to mail their inquiries.

The data base offered the publication a new opportunity to service its readers, with very little risk or cash outlay. It increased subscriptions by up to 20 percent and improved reader loyalty.

The computer spreadsheet also has the capability of being converted to a powerful data base system. The primary function of a spreadsheet is creating a grid of numbers and specifying their mathematical relationships within the grid. The relationships are tied to the locations of the numbers, not to the numbers themselves. So the numbers can be changed without changing the relationships. Viewing the grids that compose the spreadsheet as a data base rather than as a ledger, the rows of the spreadsheet become records and the columns become fields.

Infopreneurs can use their spreadsheets as a data base when in need of financially oriented information such as sorts, quick reports, and criterion-based queries. One East Coast sales executive uses his spreadsheet data base to track sales forecasts relative to the actual sales of some 200 specialty items. His first sort, by sales volume, shows which items are selling the best. He then segments, by product, which compares the actual sales figures with his forecasts. This information allows him to make vital midcourse corrections in his marketing strategy.

## Data Base Variables

Data bases are extremely valuable as collection, storage, access, and output tools. Data collection, the fundamental element in building a data base, can be expensive as personnel costs escalate. However, as storage costs decrease and storage capacities increase, infopreneurs can acquire as much information as they want. The ability to then access the data stored on file reflects the infopreneur's ability to effectively manage the data base.

Selective access of a file, known as *segmentation*, allows for targeted, personalized communications with key constituents and avoids such elaborate communications with the fringe audience.

As data collection, storage, and access make information more readily available, its output demands grow. This growth requires sophisticated management reporting to track and analyze data base activities and results.

## Data Base Construction

Data bases can be easily constructed by thinking in terms of data fields, records, and files which comprise the data base:

Data collected is arranged into relationships known as *fields*.

These fields position side-by-side geographic, demographic, and psychographic information to form a customer's *record*.

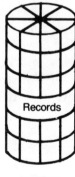

Records become files when ranked by priority based on frequency of access and need. High priority data can include names and zip codes to create account numbers. Medium priority data can be "flags" denoting exceptions, selections, or activities. Low priority data can be phone numbers, age, sex, and birthdate.

Two types of *files* created from records are flat files, magnetic tapes with limited data storage, and hierarchy files, hard disks with unlimited storage capacity.

The *data base* is known for its ability to collect, store, access, and output large amounts of information.

Functionally, data bases can be categorized as *relational* or *nonrelational*. Relational data bases allow for comparing or combining information from two or more files while nonrelational programs do not. They construct links between fields from different files which creates powerful correlations of customer activities. For example, a bank can combine the names of customers who have savings accounts and car loans through its institution. By sorting out these customers, a targeted marketing program can extend to them a line of credit for their businesses. Marketing to customers based on their recency, frequency, amount, and type of activity with the bank, reduces the risks on loans made by the bank.

One of the best applications of the relational data base management concept is in the direct marketing field where the customer/donor/client/subscriber/member becomes the measurable means to improved marketing productivity. The illustration on page 16 highlights the role of the data base relative to other media and business functions.

The first step is to collect, store, and sort the vital information of your constituency. Next, leverage your data base to discover its capabilities within your current business structure. Learn about the flexibility, adaptability, and power of relational data base management tools as applied to your current challenges. Finally, learn to place your first marketing dollar where it will bring its greatest return on investment from your data base and you will discover how easy it is to turn data into dollars.

# 3

# CUSTOMIZE
# INFORMATION

The Information Revolution has created an "information overload" that blocks effective communication. Infopreneurs help
separate irrelevant information (that which will not be useful
in making decisions) from relevant information (that which is
vital in making well-informed decisions). However, even useful
information must be systematically arranged and presented to
facilitate decision making. The problem of information overload and the need to repackage useful data have ushered in new
opportunities for infopreneurs to customize information.

Effectively customized information is based on the principle of Pareto's Maldistribution Curve. In the late 1800s,

Italian economist Wilfredo Pareto observed a phenomenon in business known today as the *80/20 Rule*. Pareto found that in many companies 20 percent of the products are responsible for 80 percent of the sales. He also found that 20 percent of the customers generate 80 percent of the revenue. Pareto's principle can be shown to carry over into the context of information management, where 20 percent of the information directly contributes to 80 percent of an organization's decisions.

Within any organization, extraction and customization of useful information occurs on three levels (see page 37):

- *Operations and production*—Compiling, computing, copying, and comparing data. This is the first level, where the "number crunching" occurs and 80 percent of the information is extracted, handled, and stored.
- *Management control*—Adapting and analyzing the information to manage and supervise resources and activities. This level, accounting for 15 percent of the information used within the organization, is where data are tailored and many decisions are made.
- *Management information systems*—Synthesizing and coordinating information. On this level, highly customized information is used by senior-level personnel. Even though the information volume is less than 5 percent, the vast majority of decisions at this level are made from this data.

On the basis of these three levels within the 80/20 formula, successful infopreneurs must first identify and rank business information priorities. These priorities help infopreneurs stay in control and assist managers who are often misinformed, uninformed, or overwhelmed by data. It is not uncommon for a distraught manager to look at a stack of computer reports and exclaim, "I know the answer is in there somewhere!" Instead of insulating managers with reams of reports, customized information frees them to better understand the realities of the marketplace.

For example, one chief executive officer hired an infopreneur to rank information priorities and customize his

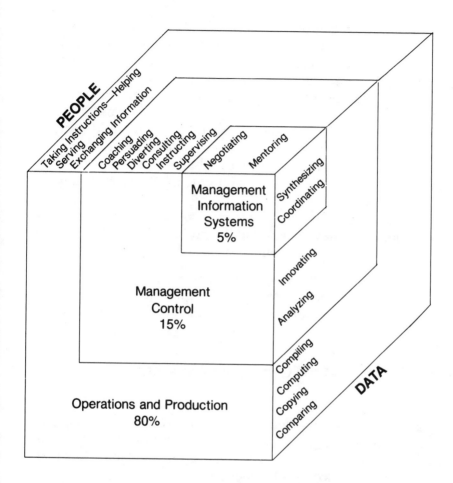

corporate data. The exercise helped answer four simple questions about the $250-million-a-year enterprise:

- What has been our past track record and the factors that attribute to this record?
- What is our current position—strengths and weaknesses?
- What factors are leading to our current strength or lack of it?
- Where are we going from here and how are we going to get there?

The answers to these questions helped this CEO effectively manage his international business.

Asking the right questions is only part of the process. Customized information should provide the answers in a form that is easy to understand. One example of customized information is computer-generated data converted into color graphics. Studies show that this type of customized information allows managers to absorb as much as three times the information as before, and in less time. In the final analysis, for customized information to be valuable, it must relieve, not create, a burden for the user. In other words, customized information should facilitate communication, decision-making, and action.

Infopreneurs do not need to be experts to customize information. Once they understand the problem before them, three benchmarks help infopreneurs succeed:

- They know where to get the data.
- They know how to sort through the data.
- They know how to present the data to decision makers.

## CUSTOMIZED INFORMATION SERVICE

At times, every business is faced with the sudden realization that it possesses inadequate data to develop a marketing plan or launch a new product. If the organization lacks the manpower or skills to obtain the required data, it must locate an outside source to meet its needs.

Andrew Garvin's FIND/SVP is such a source. As an information broker, Garvin runs an electronic research and information service. He has a business library with more than 10,000 company files and more than 10,000 subject files. Along with subscribing to more than 2000 periodicals, Garvin has access to about 1000 computerized data bases from around the country. He customizes information by:

- Conducting computer searches of on-line data bases.
- Acquiring specialized mailing lists.
- Performing library research.
- Compiling bibliographies.

- Verifying footnotes and references.
- Compiling indexes and abstracts.
- Providing clipping services.
- Retrieving and delivering documents.
- Giving instruction in research and information retrieval.

Started in 1969 from Garvin's studio apartment, FIND/SVP now has 100 employees and sales of $10 million. Characteristics critical to succeed as an information broker include an aptitude for research and flexibility.

Garvin's flexibility is apparent from the ease with which he fulfills a wide range of customer requests. When he customizes information, it can be on a one-time or a continuous basis, and the projects can range from data base research and document delivery to in-house training and written research reports.

Garvin's client requests for customized information range from obtaining information about companies involved in videotex to locating monthly articles about diabetes. He can contact a leading United States economist or provide mailing labels for executives.

Garvin conducts most of his business over the phone, rarely meeting face to face with clients.

As complex as the information business may appear, it can be broken down into two basic customized services: indepth research and one-stop information. The indepth research projects are generally large information-gathering assignments requiring primary research through questionnaires or surveys. The second type of service is one-stop information which is providing information in a matter of minutes or hours. While indepth research may be contracted out on a project basis, one-stop information can be priced as part of an annual retainer agreement or on an hourly basis.

The Information Revolution has become known for the enormous amounts of information being generated. Yet it is infopreneurs like Andrew Garvin who, for the first time, can collect, analyze, classify, then customize this information in an efficient manner that attains value in the marketplace.

One reason for Garvin's success is the complexity of the

Information Age. In order to run a successful business, owners and managers need to know more about business than ever before. Another way to view Garvin's service is that he helps customers seize opportunities and manage problems rather than simply providing information.

Garvin does not guarantee that he can provide answers to all his customers' requests, but if the supporting data exist and are not proprietary, he can usually resolve almost any information dilemma placed before him. Access to information through today's technology, and the ability to successfully customize this information has made Andrew Garvin a pioneer of the Information Revolution.

## CUSTOMIZED RESEARCH SERVICE

Charles Cleveland built Quester into a $2.5-million-a-year customized information service by analyzing key words of respondents. Whereas many research companies discourage people from giving their own unsolicited answers to multiple-choice questions, Cleveland actually encourages verbosity. He then customizes the information to solve the problems of his clients.

Cleveland began Quester in 1977, when he converted from a statistician and social psychologist at Drake University to an infopreneur. He is considered a maverick in the research arena, where the multiple-choice format is king. Yet, Cleveland's blue chip customers pay up to $100,000 for his customized research.

Cleveland set up his research center in a suburban office outside West Des Moines, Iowa. His 75 full-time and part-time researchers conduct open-ended telephone interviews encouraging interviewees to share their views on various topics. The phone conversations, which last an average of 20 minutes, are transcribed overnight and fed into a computer that recognizes up to 99 percent of normal, everyday English (50,000 words). Word usage is statistically analyzed to determine what ideas are operating in an individual's thinking. The sentences in which key words appear are also examined. Cleveland then customizes the information for his clients by using semiotic analysis—the study of words, signs, and symbols—interpreting the data and reporting his findings. He has shown:

- A major greeting card manufacturer how to design cards for women, given by men.
- A utility company which words to avoid in its correspondences.
- A savings bank how to get its customers to use its automated tellers.

The customized nature of Cleveland's information is highlighted by recurring distinctions that might otherwise go unnoticed. His reporting of these themes can be vital to a company's successful communications with its constituents. For instance, one bank hired Quester to review its advertising campaigns. The bank had advertised that its checking accounts "pay interest." Quester's interviews revealed that respondents generally associated the words "pay" and "interest" with their own activities of activities of paying bills. Customers understood this meant that they have to pay interest on the balance of their checking account. Cleveland did not overlook this nuance and suggested that the bank take another approach. In the revised advertising campaign, the bank stressed that customers "earn" interest on their accounts. The new campaign improved communication of the bank's services.

Cleveland's incisive use of the computer enhances the value of his research. The computer's ability to rapidly assess volumes of relevant and tangential information allows Quester to collapse the time frame for formulating its recommendations from weeks to a matter of hours. The computer is programmed to read data literally. Infopreneur Charles Cleveland analyzes, then customizes the information, which often leads to research breakthroughs.

Cleveland has also designed standardized communication research services to companies that are in the process of developing new product concepts. The first part of this process is to write down what the product concept is, how the product is positioned, and what the expectations are in the minds of consumers. Quester helps clients find out semiotically, or through words, signs, and symbols, what happens in the minds of consumers when they get the concept statement as stimulus.

Quester has helped clients revise and refine concepts and to reposition concepts in one-third of the time it normally takes to prepare a product concept for market. The ability to use the concepts means the product goes on the shelf in the consumer's words, from the consumer's point of view, with a motivated consumer, in significantly less time than with any other presently known procedure.

## CUSTOMIZED POSTAL SERVICE

In 1983, 26-year-old Jack Ellis started the Post Box in the heart of Annapolis, Maryland. Ellis' underground office is located directly across the street from the U.S. Postal Service. Ellis took the location to show that he could outperform the well-entrenched institution with customized information services. The Post Box seems to be simply another address to which the U.S. Postal Service delivers. It is only after the mail arrives from across the street or when his customers contact him that Ellis' customized services begin. The Post Box:

- Rents 266 post office box "suites."
- Takes phone messages for customers.
- Makes photocopies.
- Sends telex and facsimile messages.
- Engraves signs.
- Provides a notary public.
- Sends Western Union messages.
- Receives air freight deliveries.
- Provides passport pictures.
- Makes keys.
- Wraps and mails hard-to-send packages.
- Sells packing materials.

At first, Ellis felt a little like the ficticious lonely Maytag repairman. He sat hour after hour in his subterranean headquarters watching the feet of potential customers walk by. Since his Post Box generated gross sales of only $500 per month at the start, Ellis had to work nights to make ends meet. Things were often so quiet, Ellis would sleep during working hours.

The Post Box was a new concept that required public education. Since Ellis had a small advertising budget, people were not quite sure what he did. But it was his *Post Haste* sideline for Christmas-time shoppers that really gave him needed business exposure. From his booth in the shopping mall, Ellis sold shipping boxes and mailing services. Although he lost money on this seasonal service, it helped educate the public about his enterprise and turned the business around.

In less than three years, gross sales of this private post office/office services firm surpassed $13,000 per month, and Ellis was named Maryland's "Young Entrepreneur of the Year" by the Small Business Administration.

Ellis differentiates his Post Box from the U.S. Postal Service by offering customized information services. For example, those who rent his post office boxes are allowed to use a prestigeous street address and a suite number rather than a post office box number. Ellis signs for packages that arrive at a renter's "suite" box. As a value-added service, Ellis tells his clients over the phone if any mail has arrived for them. This has particular appeal for out-of-town sales representatives who work the Annapolis marketplace.

A spin-off of Ellis' customized information service began when he mailed an eight-foot marlin for a local law firm. This new service, Air Crab, ships fresh steamed Maryland crabs by next-day delivery to anywhere in the continental United States.

Although acquiring an accessible location in the heart of the city's business district may have legitimized Ellis' venture, the success of the Post Box can be attributed to his persistence. Ellis became identified as the infopreneur who provides a complete selection of seemingly unrelated information services. Yet his ability to educate businesses and consumers to this new concept paid off. In a short time, The Post Box became identified as a customized postal service.

## CUSTOMIZED CLIPPINGS

Burrelle's Information Services began in 1888 by providing newspaper and magazine clippings for the rich and famous. Almost a century later, the company was purchased, in part, by infopreneur Robert Waggoner. Improving Burrelle's growth and profits required creativity and risk on the part of Waggoner. He integrated marketing and technology into the clipping service and improved its growth dramatically.

One of the first moves Waggoner made when he bought into Burrelle's was to use computers to upgrade the clipping system. Readers used an unwieldy book that contained the words and topics to look for in their scanning. Waggoner established a software package that provided up-to-the-minute management of topics electronically. Burrelle's became the first clipping service with a fully computerized reference system.

Waggoner then expanded into television and radio coverage—another first for the clipping industry. Burrelle's 800 employees now process more information than any other private or public sector organization. They cover 1900 daily and Sunday newspapers and 8000 weekly newspapers from the United States, Canada, Latin America, and Europe. They also read some 6000 professional, trade, and consumer magazines, as well as 400 newsletters. In total, Burrelle's listings cover 40,000 categories.

Corporations became clients as the rapidly changing marketplace created a new demand for customized information. Waggoner's customized information is now purchased by more than half of America's largest 5000 companies, who have realized the necessity of staying abreast of the rapidly changing market scene. Articles take from one to three weeks for delivery. Because some clients did not want to wait that long for their information, Waggoner introduced NewsExpress, a next-day service for $1500 per month. Readers in 17 cities clip articles from 38 newspapers throughout the night. Articles are forwarded to clients by facsimile before 9 A.M.

Clients give Burrelle's detailed information about their executives, competitors, divisions, and products, along with the references to watch for. Customers then:

- Dictate when they want clippings sent.
- Determine what areas they want scanned.
- Choose from a complete line of media coverage, including television, radio, UPI, AP, Dow Jones, Reuters, and the complete newspaper and magazine services.
- Utilize an information search service to retrieve information on almost any subject.

Burrelle's Information Service is the story of an infopreneur who brought an antiquated clipping service into the Information Age. Robert Waggoner integrated information technology into an information service to provide customized information to his clients overnight.

## SELF-APPOINTED ARBITER

It has never been easier for an infopreneur to take part in corporate enterprise. As America completes its shift away from a goods-producing economy (nine out of ten new jobs in the 1970s emerged from the service sector), information and communication technology has opened new doors for perceptive infopreneurs to customize information. One such infopreneur is Mark Hulbert who, in 1980, began the *Hulbert Financial Digest*. This monthly newsletter ranks investment advisory newsletters according to their performances—a first-of-its-kind customized information venture.

At age 24, and without financial newsletter experience, Hulbert declared himself the scorekeeper and arbiter over the investment advising community. Three years later, the *Hulbert Financial Digest* had acquired 7500 subscribers at $135 a year. Because it is the most frequently quoted financial rating service, Hulbert's customized information has become an industry standard, the "Consumer Reports" for investors.

The idea for a newsletter came to Hulbert after his graduation from Oxford. As an economic analyst, he studied many of the advisory newsletters on the market and isolated one common trait: Editors of financial investment newsletters all boast about their superior stock picks. Hulbert decided to differentiate his newsletter from the hundreds on the market by simply grading those newsletters which tout investment advice. Hulbert designed his newsletter both to rate the results of predictions of investment gurus and to show the impact of their advice. He programmed his personal computer to monitor the recommendations of market newsletters, create portfolios of hypothetical investments, and calculate what was earned or lost in the month following the recommendations.

When Hulbert monitors a new financial newsletter he has his computer divide an imaginary portfolio equally among the recommended stock picks. Hulbert's computer divides the portfolios equally among the stock picks only in the event the newsletter does not have a specific model portfolio; if it does, Hulbert follows it. In other words, if a newsletter has a "Recommended $50,000 model portfolio" (as several do) and recommends buying 100 shares of stock XYZ and 500 shares of stock ABC, Hulbert's computer carries it out. The equal division of the portfolio comes only when the newsletter does not have a recommended model portfolio, which forces Hulbert to construct one for the newsletter. He reports to his subscribers the results of the investments on a monthly basis.

The growth of the financial newsletter business has resulted from the ever-widening demand for new kinds of competitive information. The *Hulbert Financial Digest* is the primary means for sorting out the winners from the losers. Hulbert is successful in this market niche because his customized information provides clarity, consistency, and impartiality in its evaluation of financial advice.

## CUSTOMIZING INFORMATION

Infopreneurs tend to customize their information in three basic formats: personalized, categorized, and generalized presentations.

## Personalized Information

Infopreneurs providing specialized information to clients consider it a personalized service. The personal approach to customized information requires the infopreneur to directly and specifically address the needs of the customer.

When a former military pilot founded the Pilots and Passengers Association (PPA), he matched amateur pilots who were short on money with passengers looking for a trip. With this service passengers get where they want to go for about the same cost as driving. The cost of flying with PPA-arranged flights is about 15 cents per mile compared to 85 cents on a commercial flight. Since passengers share the cost of operating the plane, the pilot can fly it at little or no additional cost. Pilots gain additional hours of flying time without footing the full cost of the flight.

Although the personalized information service was a good idea when introduced as a newsletter, problems arose with the lack of timeliness and inaccurate information. The service was revitalized by integrating a computer and a toll-free number. Passengers now call the PPA and a computer operator makes an instant match for a trip. To cover the costs of the personalized information service, passengers pay a $50 fee to join and pilots pay $100.

Another example is the selling of information to and on political candidates. Political Action Committees (PACs) generate more than $100 million a year in contributions. With all this activity PACs are being formed on a daily basis. And the product they buy and sell—personalized information.

PACs suddenly emerged in 1971 when an AFL-CIO amendment to the Federal Election Campaign Act made it possible for labor and other groups to donate to candidates seeking federal office. Today thousands of political action committees take the form of groups, employee funds, labor and trade associations, professional organizations, lobbyists, and backers of single issues.

One infopreneur personalizes his political action information four different ways: A data bank to PACs looking for candidates that sympathize with their goals, a data bank that allows candidates to identify appropriate PACs to finance their causes, a service that helps form Political Action Committees, and an annual encyclopedia that contains PAC statistics and "how-to" hints.

When selling customized information, infopreneurs should keep these ten tips in mind:

1. Know specifically the types of information your customers need. Be informed about what is available so you can meet this need.

2. Ask questions about the information so that you can clarify any uncertainty.

3. Don't be afraid to ask for payment in advance on the information purchase. Remember, once your customers have the information, they will begin using it to make money for themselves.

4. When your customers know the exact information they want and don't feel they need your help, encourage them to obtain the information on their own. When they need help, they will call.

5. Don't buy unnecessary information and don't neglect information you need for your own resources.

6. When you sell customized information, make sure your customers know how they plan to use the information to do more for less.

7. Prepare your "infopitch." Know the answers to questions about your information before they are asked by customers.

8. Be careful not to offer outdated information. It will probably be of little value to the customer and will not result in repeat business.

9. Be prepared to document information quality and sources in writing. Customers may even ask for a performance guarantee on the information purchased.

10. Finally, ask for referrals from your customers. The quality of your customized information is reflected in

the number of new and repeat information customers coming through your door.

## Categorized Information

The second type of customized information is categorized according to a specific need of the buyer and tends to be packaged in a "how to" format. For example, the largest selling newsletter in America is *The Contest Newsletter*. It was started by an infopreneur whose hobby was trying to win contests and sweepstakes.

One day he categorized his insights and started to promote them in a newsletter which includes:

- The methods and procedures for playing contests guaranteed to give the subscriber an edge when entering contests.
- Lists of sweepstakes and contests which one person cannot feasibly research and enter on his or her own.
- The rules and prizes, along with unraveling of ambiguous and confusing language.
- Tips that improve the subscriber's chances to win.
- Answers to questions or solutions to puzzles.
- Updates about how contest judging organizations operate.
- Interviews with other subscribers as to how they won.

Another example of categorized information is a bookstore which carries only business books. The store offers 3000 books, including more than 50 titles published by the infopreneur under the name of Caddylak Systems Book Center in New York. Customers that buy from this bookstore tend to be executives looking for information which will help improve their job performance.

Categorized information is also creatively offered by a former stockbroker who scouts out undervalued stocks, such as small over-the-counter stocks, and publishes his information in a looseleaf compendium of reports called the *Unlisted Market Guide*. In its first year, this infopreneurial venture obtained more than 1000 subscribers who paid $150 per year for the guide, while corporations paid $750 to be profiled.

This infopreneur's guide actually undercuts the price of *Standard & Poor's Profiles of the 1,000 Most Actively Traded Issues* by nearly two-thirds. His categorized information serves a very useful purpose in that many traders react more to the activity of the stock rather than such basics as industries the companies are in. The guide tracks the stock while providing basic industry background.

Categorized information must either fill a void in the marketplace or create a niche then exploit it. Once categorized information has found its way to buyers, try to quantify its perceived value by rating it.

For the information to rate "satisfactory quality" it must meet the customer's expectations for its utility. However, when the information is perceived as ideal, it not only solves the customer's problem, but also provides ancillary benefits such as new insights or new services.

One of the major advantages of categorized information is the ability to reproduce it on a large scale. Yet because of its nonpersonalized format, categorized information must still exhibit a high standard of quality (exceeding the customer's information expectations) to be long-lived in the marketplace.

## Generalized Information

More closely related to categorized information than personalized information is the third type of customized information—generalized information. Noted for its observations rather than specific recommendations, generalized information is playing a vital role in today's fast changing world.

One example of generalized information is an unusual newsletter called *Foreign Intelligence Literary Scene*. With the sharp increase in coverage of covert activity, a 30-year veteran of the Central Intelligence Agency created a 12-page newsletter that approaches intelligence from a scholarly and nonpartisan posture. This literary vehicle allows subscribers to openly read, write, and talk about intelligence from a generalized information context.

This infopreneur has helped define intelligence as a sophisticated and permanent field of human and political activity.

The newsletter varies in content and coverage, but includes bibliographies, book reviews, and brief accounts of magazine articles about intelligence.

Another example of a generalized information service is the *Issues Management Letter* which uses a complex computerized tracking system to pinpoint what issues are rising and falling in the national media. The infopreneur publishes his findings in a biweekly summary report to subscribers. The generalized information reveals, for example, which popular issues of the recent decade are being replaced by other concerns.

This type of measuring system is similar to one used by infopreneur John Naisbitt in producing his best seller, *Megatrends*. The major difference is that *Issues Management Letter* monitors activity through the national media rather than through local news conduits.

The *Issues Management Letter* has more than 175 clients who pay $275 annually for the letter and one hour of consulting. This generalized information source tends to be followed closely by corporate public relations directors.

Generalized information is being subscribed to by more companies as they monitor trends to isolate new opportunities and dangers in the marketplace. Success depends on the infopreneur's ability to translate unintelligible data into useful, strategic information.

## CUSTOMIZED INFORMATION PARAMETERS

Over the past 25 years, organizations have gone to a great deal of expense to develop systems that generate up-to-date information. Yet relatively little effort has been devoted to tailoring this information, resulting in an information-saturated environment. Within this business realm, information is often:

- Easily lost or destroyed.
- Buried under large amounts of data.
- Absorbed by other data.
- Manipulated to affect its validity.

- Diluted with irrelevant facts.
- Used in ways for which it was not intended.
- Rendered ineffective if time-sensitive.

As the Information Age places more information in the hands of more people, customized information will help infopreneurs:

- Track progress toward long-range objectives.
- Monitor the impact of environmental changes.
- Reduce energy consumption.
- Isolate cost-saving opportunities.
- Allocate resources to achieve corporate efficiency.
- Enhance customer service.
- Improve organizational performance through planning and control.

Even though customized information by infopreneurs can help management perform many vital tasks within an organization, it cannot replace managerial judgment, nor can it provide the context to make infallible decisions. It is here that the infopreneur bridges the gap.

To customize information, infopreneurs must first understand organizational needs and goals and then order them by categories such as the following:

- *Management*—Negotiations, chambers of commerce, contracts, environment, economic indicators, insurance, law, legislation, public relations, personnel policies, projections, trends.
- *Market research*—Corporations, exports, projections, reports, sales, trends.
- *Sales*—Advertisements, corporations, costs, customers, deliveries, manufacturers' representatives, procurements.
- *Accounting*—Banks, financial statements, ratios, SBICs.
- *Production*—Commodities, corporations, energy, imports, labor, manufacturers, safety, shipping, supplies.
- *Personal finance*—Investment companies, mutual funds, research, securities, stock exchanges.

Next, infopreneurs must identify all potential sources of information and then rank order these sources, concentrating only on the most relevant. The challenge to the infopreneur is being cognizant of all sources of information, such as:

- Data bases (public and private).
- Government source documents.
- Printed materials (newspapers, periodicals, books).
- Television and radio.
- Advertisements and promotions.
- Seminars and workshops.
- Libraries.
- Organizational knowledge and experience.

The infopreneur then collects and stores the information, using such electronic storage systems as: computer tapes, disks, microform, videotapes, and optical disks.

These types of systems allow the infopreneur to retrieve and analyze data in a timely manner, and to disseminate these data to customers in a usable format.

Finally, the infopreneur determines how the organization can apply the information, then classifies it according to function and role.

In short, infopreneurs customize information by following four basic steps:

Step 1: Categorize organizational information priorities by needs, problems, goals, and strategies.

Step 2: Identify all possible sources of information.

Step 3: Collect information and store it electronically.

Step 4: Determine how the organization can apply the customized information to enhance its existing information system.

Infopreneurs who customize information must consider it a resource as valuable as capital, personnel, and facilities because it costs money to acquire, process, store, distribute, and protect. When customized information improves decision making and productivity, invariably the infopreneur turns data into dollars.

# FACILITATE ACCESS TO INFORMATION

Today massive quantities of data, random facts, and isolated communications have constituted a desperate search for meaningful information. This information explosion is highlighted by the proliferation of scientific articles. In 1986, between 8000 and 10,000 articles were written each day. By 1990 the number of articles will double. Infopreneurs succeed in the information industry when they facilitate access to information in a form and context useful to their customers. Yet the discipline of information access is a relatively new phenomenon.

The Department of Commerce has tracked America's

information sector for over a century. Their figures show that it accounted for 5 percent of the workforce in 1870. In the 1950s the information sector accounted for one-third of the workforce. In the 1980s more than half of all employees work in the information sector. Although more people handle more information than ever before, the problem remains how to find the right information in a timely manner.

The increase of information activity has been monitored by indexes from 17 major information media. During the 1960s and 1970s, these indexes registered a sharp acceleration in the transmission of information while accompanied by a decrease in the amount of information consumed. Today more information exists and consumers are demonstrating limits to the amounts of information they can consume.

America's information overload context implies two trends:

- Information producers face greater competition for their products, and
- Consumers will become more discriminating as they decrease their information consumption.

Facilitating access to information in an information overload arena requires a new way of thinking about information. Knowing how to find information becomes just as important as knowing what to look for. The two basic information sources are mass media and point-of-contact media. By far, the greatest information flow is through the mass media, which includes television, radio, records, tapes, education, newspapers, magazines, books, and direct mail. Yet the fastest rate of growth is registered in the point-of-contact media, which includes data communications, telephones, facsimiles, mailgrams, first class mail, telegrams, and telex.

Facilitating access to information has become unwieldy because:

- Electronic technology increased data output capabilities.
- Information burgeoned when its costs decreased.
- The market's capability to generate information has surpassed its capability to consume it.
- The gap between information produced and information consumed continues to widen.

Electronic access to information provides a solution to this problem: Infopreneurs teaching the world new access techniques and information-handling skills (such as interactive retrieval, long distance communications, and intelligent records processing) to help obtain vital information.

Electronic processing allows infopreneurs to access desired information in less time with less paper than other methods. So infopreneurs can then spend more time on the phone with clients.

Information handling requires self-imposed priorities and limits. Infopreneurs prevent information toxicity when they differentiate for consumers between what is valuable and value-added information from what is extraneous and excessive information.

Finally, controls over how information is reconstructed and disseminated to clients requires infopreneurs to exercise good judgment. As was stated earlier, an Industrial Age paradigm is that knowledge is power. Today knowledge is not power. Instead, knowledge about knowledge is power. In the Information Age, knowing how is just as important as knowing what:

- Knowing how to find information.
- Knowing how to present information to clients.
- Knowing how the information will be used by clients.

"Knowing how" is the secret of infopreneurs who facilitate access to information.

## CLEARING UP

Cyrus Noe, a journalist for 40 years, believes that within every crisis is an opportunity. From this notion he began studying the problems facing the Washington Public Power Supply System (WPPSS). Noe realized that information on electric utility policy affairs and litigation was not available in any concise, reliable, and sustained form. He visualized an information service that would pull together all this information and report it in a newsletter format to clients. With this he launched his service called Clearing Up to chronicle the failures of the nation's largest issuer of tax-exempt bonds in its attempt to build five nuclear plants.

Clearing Up is an information service with a weekly report, 24-hour hotline, and inquiry service that furnishes documentation from court proceedings to newspaper clippings. His service not only tracks WPPSS activities, but also other energy policy development and litigation across the Northwest, Canada, Rocky Mountains, and Pacific areas. Noe monitors such continuing stories as administration proposals to sell the power marketing administrations, emerging competition among utilities, power generating surpluses, transmission systems development, and disposition of the two unfinished WPPSS plants. Stories are selected for their policy importance to the region.

Noe facilitates access to information and adds value through his analysis for about 300 subscribers in 25 states and three Canadian provinces. They pay up to several thousand dollars a year for the complete set of Clearing Up services.

Clearing Up began when Noe built an electronic newsroom in the basement of his home in Seattle and hired two full-time and two part-time employees. With a $10,000 line of credit, Noe's biggest challenge starting up was gaining acceptance from a utility committee as an outsider and unknown quantity. Noe sent the publication free to his prospective subscribers for several months until they had a chance to know what they were buying into. But Noe's ability to provide up-to-the-minute information about WPPSS and other utilities has positioned him as the power-supply system expert.

As a long-time journalist, Noe figured there might be a market for a WPPSS-based newsletter after he helped organize a conference for utilities that signed up for WPPSS plants four and five. He figured right.

Subscribers find the publication very helpful in keeping track of complex situations. Lawyers often have issues sent by overnight mail. Clearing Up is vital to clients who are holders of defunct bonds, and who are suing the 88 utilities which guaranteed the four and five bonds. Lawyers for the 88 utilities have also become avid readers of Noe's publication.

Noe targets a market that required a certain level of detail about the WPPSS activities. He realizes that it is not exciting reading, nor is it for everyone.

Noe does not utilize mass media in his marketing plan since his market is so narrowly defined. His major marketing thrust consists of sending Clearing Up out for three to four weeks to targeted prospects.

Rates vary depending on the class of subscriber. And because it is an information service, Clearing Up bills its subscribers on a monthly basis. The service will soon be available on-line and through automated telefax.

Noe has no head-to-head competitor for Clearing Up. It is the only regional energy newsletter among many national energy newsletters. The advantage to Noe's regional approach is that he knows the issues and can provide continuity to ongoing stories.

The newsletter is unique because of the peculiar nature of the western region. It is an interconnected electric utility system. Things going on at one end affect people at the other end. Clearing Up should be a long-term enterprise, especially since attorneys for the WPPSS case predict the possibility of a "century of litigation."

In a special event, such as a crisis or disaster, information is often difficult to access. In this case, Cyrus Noe initially targeted an interested, yet small, market that would pay for a steady flow of up-to-the-minute information about the default of the Washington Public Power Supply System. From there he expanded his market to include energy and utility information from the western United States and Canada. The success of Clearing Up typifies the importance of accessibility to information to help individuals make informed decisions based on the latest facts and trends.

## INFORMATION ABOUT ENERGY

Jim Hammond consults to some of the largest corporations in the world because he can quickly and efficiently provide access to vital information. When employed by the Exxon Corporation in the early 1970s Hammond tried to access their central computers to perform analyses. He was told by the accounting department, which managed the computer system, that his job would have to wait while the computer performed their accounting, credit card, and payroll activities. Hammond concluded that the corporate computers were used simply as giant adding machines and would not be available to employees as problem-solving tools. So he placed a request to have his job performed by an outside timeshare vendor. The request was approved and Hammond structured his time-sharing program to access information from cities and towns across the nation. Hammond stumbled onto the design of the first communications network in the company.

Hammond became an information superstar on March 26, 1973 when the vice president for marketing announced the formation of a voluntary allocation program with the foreknowledge of a possible oil embargo—which took place some six months later. The program restricted the distribution of the available reserves among dealers, service stations, resellers, and industrial customers. The allocation was to be done according to how much gasoline was purchased over the previous year.

The vice president wanted an information system designed to monitor supply points where the fuel would be distributed. He wanted records kept so a report could be on his desk each Friday at 9 A.M. The allocation was to be administered by the marketing distribution and engineering group of which Hammond was a part. At the time, though, Hammond was working in warehouse automation of packaged products. When the vice president announced that he wanted a reporting program in place by April 1 (in 4 days), the systems group balked and said it would take months to design such a program that collects the data. Hammond volunteered to facilitate access to the information because he perceived a correlation between the data gathering request by the vice president and the timesharing communications network he had up and running.

Once Hammond explained that it was viable and could be

achieved in a short time frame, he went from department to department automating the manual procedures. The information helped the company manage its inventories and allocations throughout the energy crisis. Hammond also played a key role in bringing the outside computer services in-house, saving Exxon nearly $20 million in annual service bureau fees.

In 1981, Hammond left the Exxon Company to form an information consulting service. His ability to facilitate access to information helped him establish a consulting relationship with his former employer. Hammond now manages the information bureau for Exxon's industrial advertising program— the type of service normally handled by employees at corporate headquarters. He fulfills up to 6000 information requests per month.

As an infopreneur, Hammond finds solutions to problems quickly and efficiently. Timing is the secret to his success. He produces results faster than in-house services because he knows not only what to look for, but also how to find it. His costs and overhead are actually cheaper for his clients than trying to do the same work in-house.

Hammond's information niche is that he understands the needs of the petroleum industry. His staff members are petroleum people with special expertise in information systems—not information people trying to sell themselves to the petroleum industry. They have never advertised, yet are always busy.

Jim Hammond became a successful infopreneur within one of the largest corporations in the world because he could facilitate quick access to information vital to decision makers during a crisis. Proper foresight and planning helped Hammond develop the capabilities to proceed when the opportunity arose.

## ASTHMA UPDATE

From the time David and Helen Jamison became aware of their son's asthma, they tried to educate themselves about his

60

condition and treatment. They learned from the doctors who function as their primary source of encouragement and information. Yet to supplement their advice, Jamison looked in vain for a layperson's publication devoted exclusively to reporting current developments in asthma research and treatment. It was then that he decided to attempt such a publication himself.

*Asthma Update* was born as a newsletter to provide relevant information for both the ten million asthma sufferers and those who care for people with asthma. But Jamison had little start-up money, so he did everything as cost-effectively as possible to create and distribute his newsletter. He used press-on lettering, borrowed a friend's word processor, used prestamped post office envelopes, obtained a savings account at the bank to avoid business account service charges.

Jamison's initial promotional techniques also centered on bringing in the most subscribers at the least cost. These included direct mail, space ads, press releases, sample copies sent to doctors, and renting mailing lists of prequalified names.

Although Jamison could economically create his newsletter and reach potential subscribers, he could not develop credibility for *Asthma Update* based upon his credentials alone. This problem was solved when Dr. Thomas Plaut, the noted Massachusetts asthma specialist and author, became interested in the benefits *Asthma Update* would have for the asthmatic community after he received a copy from Jamison. Dr. Plaut now serves as medical consultant to *Asthma Update*, commenting on selected abstracts and providing written contributions from time to time. Together Plaut and Jamison help readers of *Asthma Update* avoid emergency room visits and hospital admissions by learning how to manage asthma at home.

Even though asthma information has always been available through the Asthma and Allergy Foundation, books, and journals, easy access and selection of pertinent information has not. Jamison facilitates access to this information by tapping into more than 2500 medical journals and periodicals from around the world at the National Medical Library in Bethesda, Maryland. He then selects the most relevant information for his subscribers in this groundbreaking quarterly publication.

To arrive at a price for *Asthma Update,* Jamison analyzed which market he was trying to target—consumers or professionals. When he decided on the consumer market, he priced it on the basis of what a typical subscriber would deem reasonable. Jamison's four-page newsletter costs $8.00 for a full year.

Jamison's desire to access obscure information on asthma resulted from his own interest in the answers. The need to locate pertinent information among the thousands of articles written each day and the ability to market this information has helped David and Helen Jamison successfully facilitate answers for asthma sufferers nationwide.

## INSTANT ANSWERS

Ken McNulty, owner of Data and Research Technology Corporation (D.A.R.T.) in Pittsburgh, Pennsylvania, has created The Answers: Machine—a public pay terminal that allows business people on the road to read their electronic mail, relay information to their home offices, and tap into data information sources. He plans to do with information what McDonald's did with hamburgers—make his product cheap and available almost everywhere.

McNulty runs a small family business which has been in the computer, telecommunication, and research field since 1965. He spent nearly three years designing seven prototypes until he finally developed his system. The software he wrote is geared to the mass market at the retail level. McNulty realized the public had access to the voice network through pay telephones. What he wants to give them is access to the data network by placing them directly into the information business. For a fee of $24,000, D.A.R.T. supplies people with an IBM PCXT, software, and The Answers: Machine mechanisms.

Besides tapping into data bases, users can access the computer for word processing, spread sheets, programming, and sending mail. D.A.R.T. subscribes to data bases, and those who subscribe to D.A.R.T. access the same data bases, then are billed for the time on their accounts.

The Answers: Machines are appearing in some hotel and motel lobbies around the country as McNulty rides the crest of the information wave with his unique way to access information. McNulty has also customized The Answers: Machine so it accepts different national currencies. This conversion capability has created a worldwide market for D.A.R.T.'s information services. For example, the current telecommunications infrastructure allows subscribers in Argentina to tap into *The New York Times* data bank at any time.

McNulty has also introduced The Answers Club, a membership-only information-on-demand service. For $25 a year, customers receive a credit card with their names and access numbers on it. They can call D.A.R.T. to access The Answers: computer 24 hours a day, and ask it to do a wide variety of information searches. Club members are then billed for the cost of the search.

McNulty sees large bookstore chains, libraries and hospitals as prime markets for The Answers: Machines and related services. These operations can justify the expenses because they will use the computer for in-house needs while also profiting from their customers' use of the equipment to access information.

McNulty's service will make infopreneurs an international phenomena as his machines facilitate access to information worldwide.

## INFORMATION GURU

In 1975, a friend asked Matthew Lesko to find out why the price of Maine potatoes was double the norm. The process of answering that question became the key to tapping valuable information sources, and helped Lesko carve out his niche: a conduit through which government resources become accessible to the American public.

Lesko started his career in information services by delivering *The New York Times* to Washington, D.C. subscribers. He studied computer science in graduate school and eventually started his own software business, which soon failed. His next venture, which also failed, was an information service for American citizens overseas who wanted to return to the United States. Then Lesko started Washington Researchers— an information service that required only a desk, a phone, and a network of informed bureaucrats. Washington Researchers became a multimillion-dollar venture that provides clients with government information.

Lesko thrives on making government information accessible. Since the government rarely advertises its information resources, most consumers are unaware that such information is available. Lesko believed that the increasing amount of government information would lead to a wider gap between information generated and information disseminated.

Lesko made more government information more accessible to more people when he compiled *Information USA*, which informs citizens of government resources available to them. Lesko takes his crusade cross country in his "Info-Van" distributing information about government freebies. Lesko became popularized as an infopreneur when he disseminated to the media, clients, and prospective clients a free newsletter identifying the government as a vast information resource. The media took note and produced thousands of dollars in free publicity for Lesko, *Information USA*, and Washington Researchers.

Lesko used his own book to obtain the information needed to run a day care center; convert a business to a franchise; obtain free firewood for his home, free manure for his garden, and free fish for his pond. The information was all compliments of the United States government and typifies Lesko's ability to facilitate access to increasing amounts of useful government information.

## FACILITATING ACCESS TO INFORMATION

In the information overload context of America's society, infopreneurs facilitate access to data through eight basic market orientations which include financial, corporate, consumer, services, goods, political, education, and special situations.

## Financial

Homebuyers have a more efficient method to shop for home loans thanks to an infopreneur at CompuFund, Inc. After installing a computer to handle the paper work for 130,000 warranties, this perceptive infopreneur then checked into the mortgage information field and found that no service updates home loan terms on a daily basis. More than 100 banks, savings and loans, and pension plans now provide their latest home loan rates and terms through CompuFund—within four hours of any rate changes. This home loan data is then furnished to real estate brokers through the same terminals used to access multiple listings.

For a $100 hook-up charge and a monthly service fee of $75, real estate officers can provide a comparison of various loans available to homebuyers matching financial circumstances to desired terms—within a matter of minutes. The computerized network also delivers the loan commitment reducing the loan approval period from the industry average of six weeks down to just two weeks. Because home loan rates change on an average of every eight days, the system is programmed to automatically facilitate access to the best financial program available.

## Corporate

When an infopreneur heard presidents of multinational corporations describe their confusion over whom to contact when doing business in foreign countries, he started publishing worldwide directories of government, economic, trade, defense, and financial authorities.

Corporations pay between $250 and $650 for nearly 1000 pages of information in the form of brief historical perspectives on 171 countries. The worldwide directories by Lambert Publications even facilitate access to information on who reports to whom in each country along with telephone and telex numbers of government officials.

## Consumer

The entrepreneur who made a small fortune on Wacky Wall-walkers (more than 75 million of these small gummy octo-puses now adorn the walls and windows in the United States) became an infopreneur when he set up his Fad Hotline. This free hotline facilitates access to financing, promoting, and marketing information for people who have "something that everyone wants yesterday, yet nobody wants tomorrow."

The Fad Hotline, a toll-free number whose alpha translation spells 1-800-USA-FADS, received more than 2500 calls in its first six months. Personal advice is given to about a half-dozen callers who are lucky enough to talk with the famous faddist.

## Services

An infopreneur who studies private investors found that, as a group, they put as much money into small business as do venture capital firms. Yet they do so in individually smaller amounts. While venture capitalists bankroll about 3000 businesses a year, private investors finance up to 25,000 companies in a year.

When he realized that private investors do not want widespread publicity, and that many company owners need to locate potential investors, this infopreneur started the equivalent of a dating service. Through his nonprofit corporation, Venture Capital Network, entrepreneurs pay an initial fee of $100 and provide detailed information about their companies. Investors join the network at no charge. A printout matches those investors with possible ventures that might be of interest. From there, the investor and business owner are on their own. Like a dating service, this infopreneur facilitates access to information hoping to provide a compatible match.

## Goods

When an auto parts owner was unable to locate certain auto parts, he became an infopreneur by designing Auto Parts Locating Network. This information-rich network helps

66

salvage dealers locate car and truck parts they need. The auto parts information bank is also utilized by insurance companies wanting to save money by purchasing used parts.

A new information service of the Auto Parts Locating Network facilitates access to information about heavy duty truck and off-road construction equipment parts.

## Political

The infopreneur who started Lobbyist System Corporation wanted to put lobbying techniques and tools in the hands of people who previously could not afford it. LSC became the first lobbyist computer service based on personal computers. The system offers a special telephone connection which facilitates access to the latest information on committee updates and floor votes.

## Education

An infopreneur at Stanford University facilitates access to information as he teaches 14 course a year—about three times the normal load. Traditionally, professors increase their productivity by increasing the number of students in the lecture hall. However, this infopreneur uses technology to improve his productivity and access to information.

He teaches:

- "Introduction to Logic" to 100 students at a time, three times a year—by computer.
- "Foundations of Measurement"—by videotape.
- "Axiomatic Set Theory"—by computer.
- "Foundations of Quantum Mechanics"—up to five times a year in person.

The computerized courses are facilitated by teaching assistants who answer questions about the material presented in the courses. These teaching assistants seem to make the computer-based courses more personalized.

This infopreneur facilitates access to all material and information via computer. Students are not required to buy text books, since all of their exercises are performed on computers equipped with a theorem-checking program.

## Special Situations

Anomalous applications show infopreneurs facilitating access to information. For example, one farmer sorts through interactive networks to keep abreast of current news and market prices. The information he needs goes beyond the prices, down to the information which affects those prices, such as interest rates and the weather.

This farmer-turned-infopreneur made big profits when he picked up opportunities in the soy bean and corn markets by following global weather service, international temperature, and precipitation reports as part of tracking a drought.

Even though it requires time and money to access this type of information, his investment paid off. Information, more than ever, plays a crucial role in obtaining the supply and demand facts which directly affect this infopreneur's crops.

## TYPES OF INFORMATION ACCESSED

Infopreneurs facilitate access to information as a solution to business problems. The types of information most frequently obtained by infopreneurs through on-line services include:

- Credit and financial information—39%.
- Securities and commodities information—35%.
- Legal, medical, and professional information—13%.
- Scientific and technical information—6%.
- Abstract, bibliography, and text information—5%.
- Nonbusiness consumer information—2%.

A company hires an infopreneur to facilitate access to information because an information void exists. To facilitate access to information, infopreneurs must determine where information is not available or has become backlogged.

When infopreneurs work with business owners to facilitate access to information, they start by understanding the corporate context. Executives, managers, and business owners tend to be focused in their thinking. In other words, information must be presented in a format that provides definitive answers to problems. A concise overview of the information obtained, how it was acquired, and how it fits into their current structure are what the buyer of the information most often wants to know. Infopreneurs require tight controls over the types and amounts of information while facilitating access to it.

## WHERE TO START

The best place to start facilitating access to information is with your hobby. Gather all the information you can about this hobby. Create records and files. Write things down or record data electronically so you can begin to see interrelationships among the ideas and data.

Next, build your own network. Establish a link with other knowledge workers. Send them fact sheets about your information specialty.

Once you start getting paid for your information, then approach business owners, managers, and CEOs. They hire infopreneurs to facilitate access to information to help free them to more effectively decide, act, or communicate.

The following steps should help you prepare and plan to become an infopreneur who facilitates access to information.

1. Make information management your top priority.

2. Understand the management issues which relate to information overload.

3. Monitor all advancements and breakthroughs in applications of technologies that facilitate access to information.

4. Review your client's current information management system by noting methods of accessing, filing, storing, sorting, retrieving, and distributing information.

5. Audit the operational effectiveness of your customer's current information noting areas that may require upgrading, expansion, or enhancement of information resources.

6. Specifically identify the types of information your client desires. Be sure to understand why it is needed (competition analysis, new product introduction, etc.).

7. Provide your client with information in a concise format so it is clear and easy to understand.

8. Outline the measures your client should take to protect this information from loss, tampering, or destruction.

9. Reinforce the value of your role in facilitating access to information by quantifying your efforts on behalf of your client. Try to establish a return on investment factor in time and resources saved, as well as opportunities seized.

10. Make recommendations which will introduce more efficient ways to access and manage information among upper and middle managers.

## A LOOK AHEAD

The Industrial Age was known for its goods production. The Information Age will be known for its ability to organize these goods and the ideas used to produce them. As information becomes a resource in itself, people will need to learn new ways to view the information resource. The computer and the telecommunication infrastructure represent one of the world's most effective productivity raisers. They will be the keys to the biggest industrial change of the next few decades: The developed world's shift to an information economy.

One example of this dynamic involves Dial Info, a developer of interactive telephone/computer telepromotions. They use a computer for their clients' promotions to simultaneously access up to 1000 telephone conversations or 300,000 calls during a ten-hour day.

Another example of facilitating access to information through the infrastructure is in the use of on-line data bases. Not only can they help access information, but they eliminate duplicate research; introduce the exchange of new ideas, services, and technologies; help support the development of long-range plans; simulate economic scenarios; close the gap between buyers and sellers; identify support for a broad range of problem-solving situations.

Consider for a moment that the amount of information available today will double within the next four years. The need for disciplined information access will more than justify its role in the business marketplace. Practically every scientist has been reduced to the point of just trying to cope with the amount of information being generated, let alone comprehending it. One infopreneur developed a series of techniques for these scientists whereby they can access information that is not only relevant but actually worth reading. He uses an editorial peer-review process that weeds out the less valuable articles before they are published. He then produces only the cream of the published information for his clients.

Another approach to the problem of the information overload is offered by a "low-tech" infopreneur whose Financial Information Center houses racks of brochures, prospectuses and applications from about 50 companies, including mutual funds, insurance companies, mortgage bankers, accounting firms, and banks. Shoppers can browse among the racks, watch the Financial News Network on a giant screen, or check on stock prices using a stock-quote machine. He even offers a bank of telephones with toll-free speed-dial numbers to service representatives of those 50 companies. He simply charges companies $125 a month rent for space in a four-foot-high rack.

Companies are also getting customers to talk back to them as a means to facilitate access to information. By offering toll-free phone numbers, consumers are encouraged to call at

71

the slightest hint of dissatisfaction over a product or service. In a survey of 700 companies, nearly half had established toll-free numbers for complaint handling. Toll-free and local telephone numbers are commonly seen for anonymous tips to stop crime and catch spies. They all work under the same principle—facilitate access to information.

The infopreneurs who successfully facilitate access to information are recognized by the following characteristics:

- They are skilled technicians with the ability to instantly access hundreds of data bases.
- They consider information a corporate asset to be quantified and accounted for on the balance sheet.
- They understand the synergistic impact of information and actually suggest to clients how to get the optimum impact from their accessed data.
- They have on-call information resources which provide instant answers to 80 percent of their requests.
- They are organized and constantly on guard against information overload.
- They continually search out fresh information to update aging data.

As more information exists, more people will drown in data, random facts, and isolated communications. The most successful infopreneurs will be knowledgeable about what information their clients need, how to find this information cost-effectively, and how to format this information to facilitate communications, decision making, and action. These infopreneurs will reap the benefits as they turn data into dollars.

# 5

# SPEED UP THE FLOW
# OF INFORMATION

The most basic function of free market enterprise has been the exchange of information. What is so different about information today is its speed of transmission. Even though infopreneurs who speed up the flow of information also facilitate access to information, it is the time-sensitive nature of the information required by the marketplace that makes their service so needed.

The following example highlights the importance of faster information:

When a New York business owner in 1845 wanted to advertise a buggy whip in a San Francisco newspaper, it took four months for the ad to reach the West Coast. Back then, the fastest and safest way to move information from coast to coast was by clipper ship around Cape Horn. Fifteen years later, the advertisement took only ten days as it went from New York to Missouri via telegram, then was carried by pony express from St. Joseph to Sacramento, and finally was delivered by steamship in San Francisco. The following year, in 1861, the advertisement arrived in San Francisco in a matter of seconds through the national telegraph system. Information breakthroughs now allow for 250,000 messages to be sent simultaneously over a single line in less than one second.

The impact of information technology on the speed of information highlights the difference between the Industrial Age and the Information Revolution. The Industrial Age railroads of the 1800s cut travel time of sales figures from Massachusetts to New Hampshire by a factor of 30—from 5 days to 4 hours. The same sales figures during the Information Revolution are sent instantaneously on-line through computers. Yet, the error rate of the data entered was 1 in 300. This manual error rate problem was solved through bar codes, which were introduced during World War II to keep track of books in the library of a British engineering firm. Bar code technology is the most accurate method of capturing information and has reduced the error rate by a factor of 10,000— just 1 error in 3,000,000 entries. Today, sales figures from thousands of remote locations can be sent, received, and manipulated instantaneously at any time of the business day, virtually without error.

Infopreneurs who speed up the flow of information accrue the following benefits:

- Information can be generated, sent, and received instantaneously.
- Distance and geographic barriers are eliminated.
- Early signs of trends can be easily identified.

One information-rich company has instituted a telephone loan application and approval system that changes the way its customers finance real estate investments. In just one phone call, a loan officer gathers the pertinent data, completes the application, and approves a conditional commitment of funds, terms, and interest rates. The program reduces the time required to process the loan, centralizes the vital information (eliminating the need for a costly network of local offices), and immediately pinpoints problems with the loan application process.

New technology allows infopreneurs within organizations to manipulate information so as to generate new strategy options. The challenge for infopreneurs is to know what information they need before they sort through vast amounts of data. Infopreneurs use technology to speed up the flow of information in order to obtain that information in less time, using fewer resources.

To speed up the flow of information, infopreneurs need information systems with the capability to:

- Generate operations and management reports.
- Manipulate and retrieve data.
- Analyze hypothetical scenarios.
- Instantaneously generate and access data.

The design of any information management system should provide infopreneurs with the most efficient means of accessing information and define the pathways of information movement throughout the organization.

The flow of information should be organized around the "core business concept," which is the strategy that executes a company's overall mission. Too often, though, people focus on the technology rather than on the information that the technology provides. The strategic value of fast information becomes evident in organizations with a clear strategic focus and a well-defined mission.

An example of tying the information management system to the core business concept is the General Motors 1984 purchase of Electronic Data Systems (EDS) for $2.5 billion. GM stockholders wondered what the purchase of a data processing firm had to do with the production of automobiles. EDS generates faster information, which provides GM with:

- A system-wide information processing and communications network.
- Cost information not previously available.
- The ability to fully automate production lines.
- The opportunity to give customers exactly what they want in their automobiles.
- The capability to become a low-cost producer of automobiles.

Organizations are calling on infopreneurs to speed up the flow of information, thus reshaping markets and industries.


## THIRTEEN-YEAR-OLD ENERGY CONSULTANT

Tei Gordon, an eighth-grader from Corvalis, Oregon, uses his father's computer to obtain weekly climate data from the National Oceanic and Atmospheric Administration. He publishes the information in a weekly newsletter and mails it to his clients *months before* they can receive it directly from the government. Now in its fourth year of business, Tei Gordon's Energy Advisory Service has more than 100 subscribers at $47 a year. Gordon's clients include such businesses as General Mills and J.C. Penney. They depend on this information to conserve energy in thousands of buildings across the nation.

The Energy Advisory Service began when an adult friend of Gordon's suggested the idea. A computer programmer with his father's company then helped design the software for the newsletter. Gordon advertised his product in *The Energy User's News*, which has a subscriber base of 42,000 energy managers nationwide.

Each Monday at 7 A.M., Tei receives statistics from Washington, D.C., concerning degree-days in 210 cities. Used as an index of fuel consumption, degree-days are calculated every 24 hours to indicate how far the day's mean temperature fell below 65 degrees.

Tei arranges his energy information on a computer screen, prints an original, then photocopies it for his subscribers. His newsletter provides data that helps subscribers evaluate conservation measures in their buildings. General Mills, for example, uses Gordon's newsletter to study energy conservation in its Minneapolis buildings. The corporation has achieved nearly a 25 percent reduction in energy used—a savings of $13 million a year—thanks in part to energy information provided by Tei Gordon's Energy Advisory Service. Most clients have no idea that the information they purchase is compiled by a 13-year-old. Gordon's father, Richard, at first viewed the business as an educational exercise. But now his firm is helping to expand the applications of the information newsletter to a broader base of buildings.

This 13-year-old energy consultant signifies the power of faster information. During the Information Revolution the combination of a good idea and the delivery of vital information in a timely manner has created the opportunity for a junior high school student to turn data into dollars.

## DIRECT MAIL REVOLUTIONARY

In 1981 Robert Perlstein and three partners formed Dataman Information Services, Inc. to speed up the flow of information. In less than four years, more than 5000 businesses had purchased his information services. Dataman now attracts about 100 new clients each week.

During a short period of unemployment, Perlstein went to work for a direct mail firm. This initial exposure to the direct marketing industry and Perlstein's understanding of information's potential led him to launch his infopreneurial venture. The Atlanta-based information service replaces mass mailings with specific lists for specific audiences within a specified time frame.

Perlstein's research showed that when families move into a new home, they spend 8 to 10 times more money on the house within their first year than at any other time. So Perlstein started compiling names of new home buyers from public documents and selling them to companies that offer products and services by mail.

Perlstein's company hired many senior citizens to research the public files and record information about people who have recently purchased homes. The researchers also collect data from license applications, which are available for public inspection. The age, height, and weight information provides important psychographic data about the homeowner. Additional information is obtained from other public domain sources. Dataman compiles its information on these new homeowners each week.

In the direct mail industry, more than 56,000 different lists have been compiled and are available for public access. What differentiates Perlstein's lists from others is the time-sensitive and value-added information contained in the files themselves.

The information Perlstein provides is often quite detailed: slightly overweight mothers who want to lose the weight from their pregnancies, boat owners who subscribe to sailing magazines, coin collectors who trade at numismatic conventions. This type of information, when added to Perlstein's information about new home buyers postured to spend money on their homes, gives Perlstein an advantage over the direct mail industry. It is especially helpful to small business owners who wish to offer their services and products on a regional or national scale.

These companies can also utilize Perlstein's Val-U-Check program, a mailing package that contains a discount for the company's products or services. This value-added program allows Dataman to become the creative marketing arm to small business which further leverages the responsiveness of its mailing lists.

The direct marketing revolution on the horizon is an outgrowth of the Information Revolution. And Perlstein's ability to speed up the flow of time-sensitive information about new homeowners and other markets to the business marketplace makes him one of those infopreneurs leading the revolution.

# INSTANT LEGAL ADVICE

Robert Johnson is an infopreneur who provides personal injury information to lawyers regarding the worth in dollars of a life or limb weeks before his competitors. Johnson is president of Legal Economic Evaluations (LEE) which calculates the economic loss reimbursement someone should receive in a wrongful death or dismemberment lawsuit. The report is generally ready in one hour and costs about $150.

LEE's computer headquarters is located in Palo Alto, California, yet it maintains phone service numbers in New York City, Atlanta, Detroit, and Palm Beach, Florida. Johnson started LEE for law firms as a solution to the lawyer's need for fast, accurate information. Because LEE reports take only an hour to generate, the information can be in the hands of a client overnight.

Johnson's venture generates more than 4000 service calls each year to figure out the monetary cost of someone's life or limb. Typically lawyers contract with a university professor to generate this information. The fee can be as high as $2000 and take between two weeks and six months because of the professor's work load.

Johnson's service is often seasonal. Lawyers take summer months for vacation and try to settle cases with insurance companies to close out their books by the end of the year.

The LEE process starts with an interview questionnaire that looks much like a credit card application. In order to determine the cost of loss of a life or limb, Johnson records the person's age, sex, education level, pay, profession, fringe benefits, when the children will leave home, as well as race (which is crucial in figuring life expectancy).

The computer then figures out how much the individual would have earned and the impact of the economic loss now and into the future. Started in 1981, LEE has contracted with some of the largest personal injury cases including the Air Florida crash in Washington, D.C., Chicago's DC 10 crash, the fire at the MGM Grand Hotel in Las Vegas, and the collapse of the rafters in the Kansas City Hyatt Regency ballroom.

However, Johnson's most frequent cases involve figuring

the value of an injury such as a lost arm or brain damage from accidents. LEE's computers print out a nine-page report which deals with facts, not emotional content. The company's computer programs are written to reflect statistics in a neutral light. Therefore the answers are the same no matter which side requests the information.

The largest case Johnson has analyzed focused on the deaths of four people. LEE's computer reported the loss of lives cost $135 million collectively. The insurance company settled at $6 million.

Robert Johnson designed a service that could provide information to his customers in a matter of hours rather than months. Speeding up the flow of information helped Johnson do more for less and turn data into dollars.

## INSTANT CAMPUS INFORMATION

Infopreneur Jeff Moritz is president of Campus Network, Inc. (CNI) which provides America's colleges with information services, education, and entertainment through a dedicated satellite network. Moritz started his venture in 1982, and today simultaneously and instantly connects hundreds of colleges with the same information through his satellite network.

Satellite transmission allows Campus Network, Inc. to deliver telecourses, seminars, lectures, sporting events, movies, rock concerts, and television programming to its participating campuses at a fraction of the cost required to produce these events live on each campus. Detailed studies of this market showed that a $200 million per year business opportunity existed. There were hundreds of U.S. schools with millions of dollars of physical television plant lying fallow. The millions of students at these campuses could support a full time television network provided that the network fulfilled the appetites and expectations of this audience. The opportunity was comparable to the start up of CBS, when in the 1930s a young entrepreneur named William Paley looked at the assorted private radio stations across the United States. By locking them together, he formed the first network.

After researching the market for such a service, Campus Network, Inc. concluded that there was a need for a student-targeted network which has evolved into a national cable service by reaching hundreds of thousands of cable homes beyond its college market.

Campus Network's telecourses, telelectures, and data services provide a solution to the teacher shortage in specific courses. In other words, Moritz has established a new form of learning, *telecommunications literacy.*

Campus Network is a direct consequence of the FCC "open skies" deregulation of the late 1970s. The intent of this policy was to stimulate competition and growth among the information and communications industries. Today, Campus Network services 2.5 million college students.

Moritz determined that the college market maintained the ideal characteristics for his service because it is:

- Historically local with the potential to become national.
- A node for passage of key developments and information.
- An institution likely to survive societal changes.
- The business of colleges to manufacture, distribute, use, and store information.
- The end-user students who form the most information-literate group in history.

So Moritz contracted with more than 280 of the top universities to interconnect via satellite and instantly provide originally produced information, entertainment, and educational programming. Campus Network provides an answer to the complex information and entertainment needs of the large and lucrative college market while providing an industry model for the future role of telecommunications and video.

Colleges have turned to Moritz to provide top-quality information and entertainment for the 12 million college students who spend $25 billion on discretionary income beyond room and board. Moritz also provides a bridge to the advertising community which has been frustrated in its attempts to reach this 18- to 24-year-old consumer group of which 90 percent have checking accounts, 83 percent have savings accounts, and 53 percent use credit cards.

Society has always relied upon information as an important tool for growth. Technological breakthroughs spurred the development of Campus Network to move information from one point to another, instantly. Because there is value to the movement of information, speeding up the flow of information increases its value as Moritz and Campus Network, Inc. have discovered as they turn data into dollars.

## DETECTING EARLY SIGNS OF CHANGE

Jim Williams speeds up the flow of information to clients of the Williams Inference Service by integrating his unique inference technique with environmental scanning to identify early indicators of change. Williams theorized that identification of anomalies and aberrations reveals early on a pattern of behavior or change that can affect businesses and industries. If a series of anomalies is clustered in an area, a pattern may begin to emerge. The process of identifying this pattern is called "inference."

Inference involves the combination of seeing early signs of change and determining their impact. Williams does not use computer models since they require numbers based on changes that have actually taken place. Instead, he observes current anomalies and aberrations extracted from hundreds of newspaper and magazine articles on a wide range of subjects each month. While seemingly unrelated, these discontinuities create a pattern that is identified as inference. Inference then points to a new and unfamiliar reality.

Williams' inferential scanning technique speeds up the flow of information about the early signs of change. His technique uncovers information that is inherently time-sensitive and limited in its access. Clients include Fortune 500 companies, banks, insurance companies, pension fund managers, and individuals who invest the $18,000 per year for his bimonthly newsletter.

Williams bases his business on restricted or hidden information. Early signs of fundamental change are most often hidden, sometimes even purposely concealed or disguised. Waiting until change has occurred equates to lost opportunity in the business world. Inference discovers hidden changes to create an advance warning before the changes become apparent.

Recently, the Williams Inference Service uncovered rumors of a worldwide fertilizer shortage. While analysts were worried about the possibility of a famine from the lack of fertilizer, Williams spotted a little-publicized offer from a foreign company to buy fertilizer from American producers. The producers responded by offering 20 times the amount of fertilizer sought at prices 30 percent below the market prices that had prevailed. Because this could not have happened with a real fertilizer shortage, Williams declared the shortage a ploy to mask an impending fertilizer surplus.

Williams uses inference to provide clients with clues about early signs of change. Corporations use the information from Williams' newsletter to align their decisions and strategies with the emerging norm.

## SPEEDING UP THE FLOW OF INFORMATION

In today's business context, faster information is achieved in one of two ways—through technologies and through techniques, which are as different in nature and function as the left hemisphere of the brain is from the right. Among the technologies used today to speed up the flow of information, those having the greatest impact are the telephone, satellites, videodisks, television, and of course, the computer. Content analysis, environmental scanning, and inferential reading effectively provide insights into early signs of technological, economic, political, and social change.

## Technologies

### Computers

When a Heisman Trophy winner graduated from college and became a professional football player, 69 agents, lawyers, and promoters approached him offering the best in contract negotiations. Rather than interviewing each one, his father wrote a computer program that ranked each prospective agent in categories and weighted each category according to its importance. The categories took into account expertise in direct negotiation with the NFL, tax expertise, and entertainment connections, among other key factors. The computer made the recommendation, reducing the search process from months to a matter of weeks. The agent chosen successfully negotiated a multiyear, multimillion-dollar contract for the NFL rookie.

Faster information became a story in itself when a train carrying phosphorous derailed near Dayton, Ohio. A poisonous phosphorus cloud forced more than 30,000 residents to evacuate their homes. Infopreneurs at Mead Data Central, an electronic information company, sorted through its files for information about phosphorus. In less than an hour, an 80-page packet was presented to journalists with everything they ever wanted to know about phosphorus—and more.

Changes in the competitive executive search business have resulted in corporate infopreneurs bypassing the headhunters. Applicants can now send résumés directly to potential employers via computer. The speed of this approach provides a competitive edge to participants by eliminating the expense of a middleman. Employers soliciting calls via computer also provide candidates the confidentiality of two-way computer conversations.

Infopreneurs at the Carolina Freight Carriers needed a faster way to share its shipping information with customers. They created the trucking company's "Snapline" service. With the aid of an IBM PC, instant information on shipping rates and transit times is delivered to truckers. The computer system is programmed to answer up to 1000 inquiries an hour. This infopreneurial venture, which has serviced more than 40,000 customers, takes the mystery out of ratings and tariffs.

Fast information was also a major challenge to info-preneurs at the Tennessee Valley Authority. While rethinking its information delivery strategies to the public via the media, the nation's largest electrical utility set up a computer bulletin board to change the way the utility distributes information. Using an IBM PCXT, information delivery is divided into nine user areas. Members of the media can call in and receive press releases, scan copies of speeches, review agency calendars, and research utility reports. This program succeeded in disseminating more information in less time to the media.

Finally, when an infopreneur wanted to research information pertinent to her company's new product, she simply typed into her computer the following symbols: //ENCYC. Instantly she tapped into an on-line encyclopedia which offered her more than 30,000 articles to choose from.

### Telephones

Infopreneurs in the publishing industry recently began replacing reader inquiry cards with phone calls. The typical turnaround time for a reader service card from a potential buyer to the seller is about six weeks. In today's competitive marketplace, this time lag makes most promotional materials of little use. As in the case of one magazine, 60 percent of its business-to-business inquiries represent a bona fide prospect for future sales. The ability to deliver reader inquiries to advertisers within 24 hours by a Touch Tone telephone call from readers has increased the number of advertisers for the publication.

Infopreneurs within the Republican Party also used the telephone to speed up the flow of information and register two million new voters. Of the 20 million potential voters called in 28 states, most of the initial contact was made by automated telephone systems using computerized dialing devices and recorded messages. When tested against live volunteers making the initial call to voters, the recorded messages from the automatic telephone campaigns achieved the same results reaching more people in less time than its live counterparts while proving to be less expensive and easier to organize.

Finally, a 32-year-old infopreneur has introduced a tele-phone service to veterinarians in 4800 animal hospitals across the country. Once cardiogram leads are attached to dogs, cats, horses, or other animals, the electronic information is sent via telephone lines to Cardio Pet's Brooklyn headquarters. It is there that veterinary cardiologists provide instant diagnosis of the electrocardiogram.

### Videodisks

Videodisks are now offering a full range of financial services, instantly, using touch-tube technology. Shoppers in many large department stores use the kiosks placed strategically at store entrances. Shoppers, encouraged to touch the tube, enter into a video dialogue. At the right moment, the customer is asked to pick up the telephone in the kiosk, and complete their transaction with a store representative located at a telemar-keting center. Some kiosks contain credit card slots to charge merchandise sales.

One 28-year-old infopreneur has even substituted face-to-face sales calls with videodisk presentations to speed up the flow of information. When prospects called, he found it too expensive and time consuming to visit each one personally. So now he simply drops a videodisk in the mail along with instruc-tions and product support materials. A phone call is generally all that is needed to consummate the sale of his multithousand-dollar product. One advantage of the videodisk over videotape is the time element to access any picture (within about two seconds), versus viewing the entire tape.

One infopreneur recently introduced a videodisk catalog to selected department stores to speed up interior designing. An interior decorator for model homes catalogued all types of fabrics, paints, wallpapers, and carpets on videodisk. This cat-aloging allows an interior designer to sit at a terminal and coordinate a room for customers in a matter of minutes as pictures of carpeting, wallpaper, and paints are displayed on the screen.

### Satellites

One infopreneur is now using satellites to send sports infor-mation instantly to clients. He considers sports wagering and options trading the same type of challenge: It is no more of a gamble when the Redskins are favored to beat the Cowboys by six points than when investors on Wall Street speculate and purchase options. One is sold by a stockbroker and the other by a bookmaker.

So his information company, Telesports, focuses on the annual $200 billion sports wagering market. This infopreneur tracks and monitors all the variables which might affect the outcome of a sporting event. By using a satellite to transmit information, any last minute changes, such as playing field conditions or player injuries, can be transmitted instantly and simultaneously to all subscribers.

Infopreneurs at Satellite Data Corporation use satellites to transmit word and data processing jobs from Barbados in the Caribbean. The work is entered by computer workers from the islands who earn $12 a day as compared with up to $12 an hour in the United States to perform the same tasks (an example of "doing more for less"). The information produced by the Barbados workers is then beamed back to the United States via satellite communications.

### Television

Infopreneurs at the Home Computer Network recently introduced the first system to deliver computer software programs via cable television rather than through the traditional conduit—telephones. In analyzing the problems of transmitting computer software over telephone lines (it tends to be time consuming and expensive) the idea of using cable television lines proved to be an efficient alternative.

And who would have thought that people would watch television commercials 24 hours a day? Infopreneurs at the Home Shopping Club did. They have introduced a revolutionary way to shop for products which takes less time and costs less money than the traditional retail route—over the television. Buying products is completed with a single toll-free telephone call to a central ordering service. A credit card number is taken and the product gets shipped within hours of the order. The success of the Home Shopping Club is reflected in the fact that its infopreneurs are not buying airtime to promote the products; they are actually buying television stations and running their programming around-the-clock.

## Multi-Technological Application

Perhaps the greatest breakthroughs in speeding up the flow of information will occur as several technologies are integrated into the information system of a venture. For example, the chart on page 89 outlines the operational overview of an international real estate lead generation and product sales program for the nation of Israel. The primary point of contact for reaching the upper scale mass market in America was determined to be independent and cable television networks. A one-hour entertainment telecast from Israel was sponsored by the real estate developers. During the telecast, "infomercials" (information commercials) carefully edited into the story displayed a toll-free telephone number inviting interested investors to call for an information kit which included a videotape of the development.

Operators at a telemarketing center in Minneapolis, Minnesota, handled the inquiries and captured the following information: name, address, telephone number, age, whether they had ever visited Israel, and whether they wanted to purchase the video tape. Callers ordering the kit paid $25 by credit card (credited against the purchase price of their time share units) received their video tape within 48 hours.

The caller information was then transmitted electronically to a data processing service bureau in Maryland. A personalized laser letter thanked the caller for expressing interest in the time-share unit. The letter, enclosed with the information kit and videotape, was mailed by overnight mail to these qualified prospects. Two days later, trained outbound telemarketing sales representatives called these sales leads to answer any questions and secure a commitment to the purchase of a time-share unit. The sales purchase, initiated with a $295 down payment, was payable by credit card.

The appeals of this type of multimedia approach are the large number of qualified leads that can be generated, and the speedy flow of personalized information to them about the opportunity. The secret to its success is due to the fact that

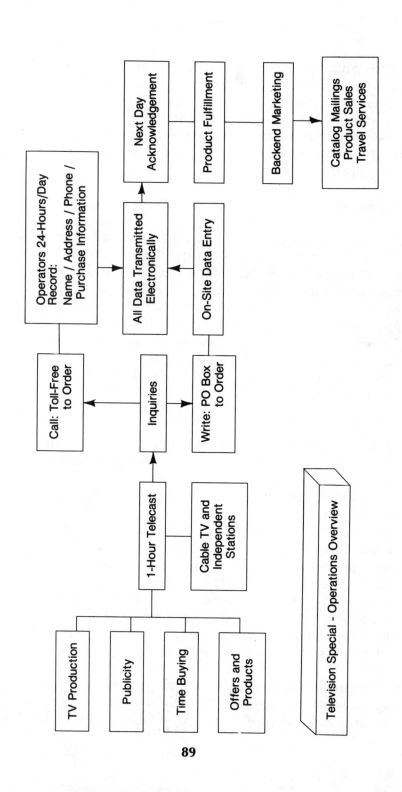

Television Special - Operations Overview

personalized information is in the hands of the prequalified caller within 48 hours of their phone call. With the point of contact for ordering the information kit being the telephone, the appropriate follow-up medium is also the telephone. This strategy minimizes the need for sales agents to personally meet with the buyers to consummate the sale—significantly reducing the sales cost.

## Techniques

In recent years, one of the qualities that has distinguished successful businesses is the ability to stay ahead of economic, social, political, and technological change. Technological expansion has forced rapid and unpredictable changes on businesses. The complexity and importance of anticipating and following early signs of change and its impact, has brought forth several new techniques to speed up the flow of information and monitor these changes. Three popular techniques include content analysis, environmental scanning, and inferential reading.

### Content Analysis

Widely read futurist John Naisbitt founded The Naisbitt Group to identify and analyze social, political, and environmental trends.

After spending 20 years with large corporations as a writer, Naisbitt developed a content analysis newsletter to report new events and changes in public behavior. From this data, he isolated the forces he felt were changing the world. Ten of these forces became the subject of *Megatrends*, which sold over six million copies in 21 languages.

Naisbitt's technique was patterned after the military's content analysis systems used for counterintelligence purposes. He reads, clips, and categorizes information from 200 daily newspapers. Naisbitt then isolates trends in relation to the amount of space they are allotted on the printed page.

Infopreneurs can speed up the flow of information by noting early signs of change through content analysis without the costs and volume of printed matter. By contracting with a newspaper clipping service, requested information can be clipped, indexed, microfiched, then analyzed for trends. A long term commitment to content analysis is required to reap its fruits as an information management technique.

### Environmental Scanning

Environmental scanning is a way of coping with emerging social, economic, and technical hazards and opportunities. Such events, when in the early stages, do not usually lend themselves to being addressed, defined, or solved by the corporation that is busy monitoring its growth and performance in the marketplace.

Environmental scanning is a strategic approach to organizational planning. Infopreneurs who speed up the flow of information through environmental scanning help their clients understand several issues:

- The level of investment required to make environmental scanning a strategic weapon.
- The types of information available through environmental scanning.
- How to integrate environmental scanning into the corporate planning process.
- The impact of changes observed through environmental scanning on the company.

Environmental scanning starts by defining how to obtain data. External data is acquired through political, legal, economic, competitive, market, technical, social, and natural sources via the print and electronic media. The second type of data, internal, can be obtained through the firm's purchasing, production, inventory, accounting, and sales divisions.

Once gathered, external and internal data is analyzed through the company's management information system, resulting in reports and recommendations to help decision makers fine tune plans and control the implementation of their businesses.

This technique, even when established in-house by infopreneurs, requires a commitment of time and resources in order to succeed.

## Inferential Reading

Although closely related to content analysis and environmental scanning, inferential reading actually depends heavily on intuition. While inference requires practice on the part of the infopreneur, it is the most cost-effective technique to start speeding up the flow of information.

Infopreneurs do not need to subscribe to 200 magazines and newspapers to work with inference. They just need to focus on anomalies. Inference, an inductive approach to the environment, starts with observations of anomalies and aberrations within the articles currently being read. For example, when the phrase, "for the first time" shows up in a sentence it can be observed as a departure from the norm, and should be considered an anomaly.

Quite often, first time events may appear to be just flukes. However, when juxtaposed with other first time activities, a pattern may be observed and its impact on the emerging order inferred. Below is a list of key words and phrases that often signify early signs of change. These words, as part of the inference process, should help infopreneurs speed up the flow of information about early signs of change:

| | | |
|---|---|---|
| introduced | challenges | is becoming |
| shift | a big | peculiar |
| have changed | a sudden | rare |
| is starting | never before | replacing |
| private | change | may soon exceed |
| most important | costly | is planning |
| cancelled | still | below average |
| the biggest | historic | surprising number |
| is being tried | new highs | will be allowed |
| can now | highest | unprecedented |
| taking the place | stepping up | significant |
| an alternative | is coming to | sharp increase |
| innovative | reversing | now features |
| an unusual | trend | greatest |
| surprising | all-time | reversal |
| a test | more directly | the lowest |

| | | |
|---|---|---|
| a surge in interest | traditionally | exclusively |
| discrepancy | unconventional | surprised by |
| extraordinary increase | in a switch | unusual display of |
| the only | record | a new product |
| increased | reduced | is coming |
| declined sharply | pioneering | cooperating with |
| unexpected | has developed | unique |

# THE VALUE OF FASTER INFORMATION

American offices processed more than 1.4 trillion document pages in 1985. The costs associated with receiving, storing, sorting, and transmitting these documents are not insignificant. One of the most important benefits of faster information is its ability to reduce the costs associated with information processing while improving productivity.

For example, infopreneurs in one venture transformed its written sales reports into electronic signals then sent them over phone lines to a central computer. Previous turnaround time for sales reports was 60 days. Data are now entered via portable teletransaction systems and reports are processed instantly. With editing of reports occurring at the source of input, this infopreneurial venture has eliminated 10,000 written report forms a week and reduced administrative costs by 75 percent. The value of faster information was realized for these infopreneurs when productivity increased while costs dropped—*simultaneously.*

The ability to transmit information faster benefits all facets of an organization which depend on the information. To speed up the flow of information, infopreneurs should ask and answer the following questions about their information needs:

- Why is the information important?
- What problem will the information solve?
- How often is the information needed?
- How does the information help achieve corporate goals?
- Is around-the-clock access to the information needed?
- Who is the source of the information?

- Where is the information generated?
- What is the most efficient way of obtaining the information?
- How can the information be stored and accessed electronically?
- What is the cost/benefit for using the information?
- What types of security are needed to protect the information?

The answers to these questions form the basis of the infopreneur's information network. Using advanced electronic information processing methods, infopreneurs gather, store, retrieve, and transfer information at a faster pace than at any other time in the history of business. Faster information facilitates better decisions, improving productivity and reducing costs, thereby providing the infopreneur with a competitive edge in the marketplace.

The information movement matrix *(see Chart p. 95–96)* helps isolate opportunities to increase the velocity of information. Quite often several options to speed up the flow of information can be generated from this type of analysis. To effectively utilize this chart, place an "X" across from the *Business Information Structure* and into the box representing the *Types of Information* being moved. Consider each option that can increase the velocity of information from among the technologies, channels, services, and packages. Then analyze its upside potential, downside risk, and steps of implementation. The result will be an infopreneur who speeds up the flow of information and turns data into dollars.

# Information Movement Matrix

|  |  | Business Information Structure | Types of Information | | | | |
|---|---|---|---|---|---|---|---|
|  |  |  | Data | Text | Image | Voice | Picture |
| Technologies | Information | • Computers<br>• Terminals<br>• Microforms<br>• Business Forms<br>• Printing & Graphic Equipment |  |  |  |  |  |
| Technologies | Integrating | • Packet Switchers<br>• Modems<br>• Facsimile<br>• Digital Switches<br>• Switchboard |  |  |  |  |  |
| Technologies | Communication | • Telephones<br>• Transmission Systems<br>• Mail Equipment<br>• Video Disc Players<br>• Radios<br>• Televisions |  |  |  |  |  |
| Channels | Communication | • Telephone<br>• Telegraph<br>• Physical Delivery<br>• U.S. Post Office<br>• Satellite Carriers<br>• Mobile Services<br>• Paging Services<br>• Cable T.V.<br>• International Record Carriers<br>• Value Added Carriers |  |  |  |  |  |
| Channels | Broadcast | • Radio Networks<br>• Multipoint Distribution Services<br>• TV Network<br>• Teletext |  |  |  |  |  |
| Services | Content | • Electronic Data Base Providers<br>• Libraries<br>• Indexes<br>• Information Brokers<br>• Data Base Distributors<br>• Videotex<br>• Non-Electronic Data Base Providers<br>• News Services |  |  |  |  |  |

# Information Movement Matrix (*continued*)

| Business Information Structure | | | Data | Text | Image | Voice | Picture |
|---|---|---|---|---|---|---|---|
| Services | Facilitation | • Time Sharing<br>• Banks<br>• Electronic Funds Transfer<br>• Ad Agencies<br>• Software Services<br>• Systems Design<br>• Management Consultants<br>• Conferences<br>• Market & Business Research<br>• Facilities Management<br>• Service Bureaus | | | | | |
| Packages | Content | • Newspapers<br>• Newsletters<br>• Loose Leaf<br>• Directories<br>• Reports<br>• Micropublishing<br>• Magazines<br>• Books<br>• Films<br>• Records<br>• Tapes<br>• Video Discs | | | | | |

# REPACKAGE INFORMATION

Infopreneurs repackage information by organizing it, then re-combining it to bring about new information products and services. This process starts with the search for a unique opportunity. Such an opportunity often lays dormant for years, because its potential has been unrecognized or undeveloped. The computer itself exemplifies the concept of delayed opportunity. All the knowledge needed to build one was available by 1918:

- Binary arithmetic was first used around 500 B.C.
- Calculating machines were designed in the mid-1800s.
- Punch cards were used for the United States Census in 1890.

- Audion tubes were invented in 1906.
- Symbolic logic was defined by 1913.
- Programming and feedback were integrated during World War I.

Yet the first operational computer (ENIAC) did not appear until nearly 30 years after the war, when infopreneurs finally pieced seemingly unrelated parts of the puzzle together.

Repackaged information products and services begins when an infopreneur performs a comprehensive search for opportunities in an area of interest. The goal is to locate as yet unrelated but possibly relatable information. New opportunities form as the infopreneur begins to analyze problems and voids within that information. Success then comes from a simple, yet focused, solution to a previously unmet or unperceived need.

The ability of infopreneurs to successfully repackage information can come about by varying their schedules or work habits:

- They learn to juggle several projects at once, enabling them to draw direct correlations from seemingly random relationships.
- They periodically disrupt the work routine in order to form new approaches, patterns, and insights.
- They try to place inconsistent data side by side with needs in the marketplaces to create new information opportunities.
- They turn unsuccessful efforts into learning experiences, to cultivate patience and knowledge.

Opportunities to repackage information are everywhere. One infopreneur with no cash wanted to create a multiclient study. She sold the idea to several companies who each paid $20,000 to $30,000 for the in-depth analysis of a certain market segment. But the real money came when she published the information and sold it as off-the-shelf market research reports, a newsletter, and promoted it in seminars and through her private consulting practice.

Another example of repackaged information is by a 25-year-old infopreneur who saw a new application of the video phenomenon: Video Yearbooks. He now teams up with students at high schools and colleges to film various aspects of campus life and produce a video version of the traditional campus yearbook.

One infopreneur actually repackages information from her clients' telephone bills to ferret out errors and overcharges. With all the regulations, most executives are unwilling or unable to find the errors in phone bills and just assume they are correct. But she finds that the phone bill is wrong in 90 percent of the cases questioned with the phone company charging an average of 10 percent too much on these bills. Her infopreneurial venture saved 400 clients more than $3 million, mostly by catching mistakes such as misplaced decimal points and duplicate billings. Her venture is strictly one of commissions. She does not charge her clients a fee, but receives half of what she recovers from the phone company.

Infopreneurs repackage information when they search for opportunities, then organize and recombine information to provide solutions to needs in the marketplace.

Finally a new information service repackages the statistics of high school baseball players to provide an evaluation tool that improves recruiting for college baseball teams. Traditionally most information about potential college prospects is carried by word of mouth. One infopreneur now provides a computer data base filled with the names, athletic evaluations, and academic records of high school players from around the country to any college coach. All the coach has to do is call the service and hook the phone up to a personal computer to get profiles of every player who fits his need.

One of the most important exercises any infopreneur can go through is an information audit to determine the role and value of the repackaged information. Some of the questions that should be asked as part of this audit include:

• How does your repackaged information provide a solution to a specific problem?

- Is your repackaged information original or an improvement on what is currently available in the marketplace?
- What type of protection do you provide for your repackaged information?
- What kind of market research have you done on your information?
- Why do you feel your repackaged information is marketable?
- How much money did it or will it cost you to repackage your information?
- How do you plan to finance this venture?
- How much do you feel that your information should sell for?
- How did you arrive at this price?
- How long did it take you to repackage this information?
- Is this your only information product or service or is it part of a larger package?
- What is the half-life of your repackaged information? In other words, at what rate does the information become dated?
- When is the best time of year to offer your repackaged information?
- Why do you feel your repackaged information will sell in today's market?

It is important to understand one final thought about repackaged information: behind every profitable venture is an active promoter of the information. Credentials are not enough with repackaged information. You have to go out and sell it as a solution to the problems in the marketplace. Learn how to take the public's pulse then repackage your information to meet their needs.

## BROADCAST INTERVIEW SOURCE

In 1984 infopreneur Mitchell Davis saw a need for a source of names for interviews on talk shows. He met with a public relations firm, which hired him to package and market the idea. Just before beginning his venture, Davis took a vacation. When he returned, the public relations firm had folded. Rather than discard the idea, Davis decided to launch it himself as the *Talk Show Guest Directory*.

Davis' biggest challenge was obtaining media recognition for his directory. Encouraged by a direct mail test campaign from which he acquired his first significant client, Davis financed his venture with $3000. The first edition of the directory was 64 pages long and included the names of 600 potential interview guests. Davis gave copies away to radio and television stations across the country; two years later, more than 3000 copies were sold to the media. The directory is updated annually. The most recent version is 384 pages long and lists the names of 3355 experts and authorities by topic. Davis' directory is now used by 82 percent of the leading news/talk radio stations nationwide.

The *Talk Show Guest Directory* unites two distinct groups: people who want to advertise their expertise and people who want interview sources for their programs.

Davis reconstructs information by soliciting the names of experts from a wide range of sources including trade groups, national associations, public interest groups, Fortune 500 companies, public relations firms, and mailing lists. He contacts the people and asks if they are available to appear as guests on radio or television talk shows and would like to be listed in a source book that is sent to hundreds of media sources. Of those that respond, 10 percent buy advertising in the directory.

Other directories have been on the market for years. What makes Davis' directory unique is the fact that it is the most comprehensive, and sells for one-fifth the cost ($19.95) of competitive sources. Davis can keep the price low because the advertising subsidizes the production costs. Davis' strategy is clearly successful, since 70 percent of his advertisers renew their ads in the directory.

Since 82 percent of America's leading talk shows are clients, Davis has reached a saturation point in his current market, forcing him to expand into new markets. To accomplish this, he has changed the name of the directory to *Directory of*

*Experts, Authorities, and Spokespersons.* The name change repositions the book and makes it useful to print media as well as broadcast media.

Davis repackages information in the talk show directory into another form: *The Talk Show Guest Directory Rolodex.* The Rolodex compatible information, which sells for $185, has been purchased by "Night Line," *Christian Science Monitor,* and *The Boston Globe.*

Davis has recently introduced a new information product called *Talk Show "Selects,"* which lists the producers of talk shows throughout America. Experts, authorities, and spokespersons who wish to market themselves directly to the programs can buy the *Talk Show "Selects"* in one of four forms: Rolodex-compatible cards, printed reports, mailing labels, or compact disks. In essence, Davis has compiled two lists (names of interviewees and names of interviewers) and markets them to each other—a stroke of infopreneurial genius.

Mitchell Davis' success in reconstructing information is in part due to the fact that he asks the right questions. For example, his last solicitation for the *Talk Show Guest Directory* included the question "Can you produce a Spanish-speaking guest?" More than 30 percent of the respondents said yes. Davis then parlayed this information into a new directory of guests for the Hispanic market.

Mitchell Davis serves as a link between experts and the media. He has repackaged information into several forms that are used throughout the print and broadcast industries.


## REPACKAGED NEWS RELEASES

David Adler repackages information through his newspaper made up entirely of press releases. The publication, called *Immediate Release,* targets thousands of influential people in the Washington, D.C. marketplace.

This is the second publishing venture for the young infopreneur who founded a controlled-circulation magazine called *Washington Dossier.*

Adler's *Immediate Release* publication introduces a new distribution outlet for organizations trying to get their messages to the media, opinion leaders, and the general public. Public relations firms provide Adler with press releases, news photos, and advertisements, and his *Immediate Release* provides the distribution system.

*Immediate Release* charges $440 per press release page. The same press release placed on the front page costs $1760. Every Friday morning *Immediate Release* is delivered within the *Wall Street Journal* and *The New York Times* to members of the media, executives, issues managers, and government officials. Fridays tend to be the day of the week when news time slows down. Adler felt this day offered an opening for a nontraditional publication such as *Immediate Release*.

Besides being a first-of-its-kind information resource, *Immediate Release* also offers PR firms a percent rate reduction—making it like the commissionable advertising field.

Although *Immediate Release* began by reducing the press releases and running them four to a page, Adler turned to desktop publishing technology to create a look more like clippings from the morning newspaper. This service has particular appeal for news items that are not necessarily immediate in nature, due to its once-a-week delivery schedule. The niche for Adler's reconstructed information therefore is as a type of community bulletin board, providing visibility of issues for its participants.

Adler wants *Immediate Release* to create a new habit among its constituents. It offers public relations more broad-based distribution rather than the traditional targeted and personalized press release. *Immediate Release* is the option to news releases that arrive in envelopes, are opened, read, used, or tossed. Adler offers the opportunity to scan more than 50 press releases in one sitting.

The public relations community is encouraged by the new format. They consider *Immediate Release* innovative and worthwhile for the business marketplace. It also serves as a unique promotional tool for certain segments of the public relations community.

Adler invested $100,000 to launch *Immediate Release*. His return will be directly related to the publication's ability to create interest among a targeted constituency for repackaged information.

Adler recently expanded *Immediate Release* to include job listings, an about-town column, regular feature stories, events calendar, photo coverage, resource guides, and data bases. He now calls it *The Washington Herald* and it is delivered to 25,000 Washingtonians who deal with Washington as a national city. More than ever, Adler is committed to providing *freedom from the press* by giving organizations a means of stating their stories through their own news releases—*in full* and *unedited*.

## REPACKAGED LEGISLATIVE INFORMATION

The 1987 Maryland General Assembly consisted of *188* Senators and Delegates who introduced *2718* joint resolutions that were discussed in more than *600* committee hearings and massaged by *627* registered lobbyists and *590* legislative staffers who processed *2839* amendments through *4000* roll-call votes in the House and Senate to yield *913* successful bills that prompted *93* vetoes by the Governor resulting in *789* new laws in just *90* days.

At one time, under this frenetic pace, the Maryland legislature enacted an 11-page bill to regulate corporate stock takeovers. The bill passed unnoticed to the Governor's desk for signing. American Motors officials realized that the bill would outlaw routine stock transactions essential to their business. American Motors executives flew from Michigan to Maryland. They hired lobbyists to pressure the Governor into vetoing the bill. A special session was called, and a new version of the bill was passed.

Tom Basil, 28, recognized the need to monitor the volume of legislative activity. He then founded the Legislative Tracking Service to repackage this information to solve such problems.

Basil's years at the State House began before he finished

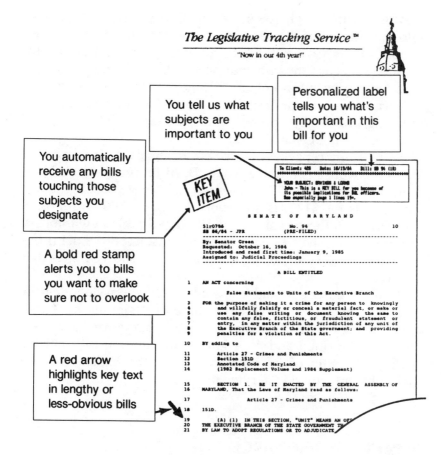

high school. As a student page in the Senate, Basil used to hitch rides with the Senate president. Upon graduation from college in 1977, he became an advance man for the Governor. Just prior to the start of his Legislative Tracking Service, Basil served as the Assistant Executive Director of the Maryland Association of Counties.

The Legislative Tracking Service monitors state legislative activities for businesses, associations, political groups, and newspapers. It keeps its clients up to date on the progress of bills that could affect their special interests. When he takes on clients, Basil conducts an extensive interview to understand their business and information needs.

Basil's formula is simple: Give clients only the information they need within 24 hours of its availability. Businesses can tap into the state's legislative computer system, but Basil's clients depend on his proven ability to cut through the clutter of activity and repackage the information so it becomes plain to them. This legislative infopreneur's $1500 personal computer outperforms the General Assembly's new $200,000 computerized indexing system by compiling more than 23,000 "yea" and "nay" votes on legislative issues.

Basil again repackages this basic legislative information when the House is not in session. Basil reorganized his information to produce *The Yearbook of Maryland Legislators,* which sells for $135. Basil spent more than 800 hours of research over a three-year period to compile this new information resource. The 636-page book is considered the definitive work on senators and delegates and the legislative issues they vote on.

Basil's exposure to and knowledge of the Maryland legislature gave him an edge when it came to designing his Legislative Tracking Service. But it was his commitment to give clients the refined and repackaged information they needed within 24 hours of its introduction by the legislature that makes his information service unique.

## REPACKAGED RESEARCH

When Daniel Stusser got fired from his job, it gave him the perfect excuse to do something he had wanted to do all along—start his own business. Stusser contacted several companies he had interviewed while writing *Profit and Control Through Call Accounting,* a business book about telephone management systems. Stusser told them that he was starting his own consulting firm and several of the companies assigned research projects to him.

One of the first projects was a multiclient study in which 11 manufacturers, software suppliers, and long distance carriers paid Stusser to research what end users wanted in a new kind of call accounting product. Each client paid $6500 for two copies of the research report. That project gave Stusser the idea of creating an industry-wide information resource for the call accounting segment of the telecommunications industry.

Since call accounting was such a small industry in 1984, no one had conducted such a study. The only people writing about call accounting back then were the manufacturers pushing their products. During his research, Stusser positioned himself as the primary research source.

Stusser was only 25 years old when he founded The Ergotec Group in 1984. Since then, he and his associates have directed several confidential research projects for such clients as AT&T Information Systems, Burroughs Corporation, Northern Telecom, Mitel Corporation, as well as dozens of call accounting, telephone equipment, and software suppliers.

Stusser, a Harvard graduate, is a contributing editor to *Teleconnect* magazine, a member of the Society of Telecommunications Consultants, and on the editorial advisory board of *Datapro Management of Telecommunications*.

Stusser repackages the raw data on the telecom management marketplace, informing manufacturers, software suppliers, service providers, and investors about:

- The size of the marketplace in dollars and systems.
- Installed base descriptions by type of telephone system.
- Sales by type, size, and distribution channel.
- New system versus replacement installations.
- Projections for shipments, by type of system, in both dollars and units.
- End-user applications.

From this research information, Stusser generates and maintains profiles of more than 150 competitors including information about products, distribution plans, national account programs, and new product plans. He is careful to publish only publicly available information so as to maintain relationships with virtually every company in the industry.

Stusser's repackaged information is bound into a hardcovered book entitled *Call Accounting Markets and Competitors* and priced at $2500. Stusser priced this information product by considering its relative value: He figured that an inside market researcher, being paid $2500 per month could not come up with a similar report even when devoting a full month to the project.

Purchasers of the 280-page report may also schedule Executive Briefing Sessions—a series of one-day meetings—with Stusser for an additional fee of $900 plus travel and expenses.

Once the information was gathered and repackaged, it became a strategic planning tool, a marketing resource, and an industry perspective for those participating in the telecommunications markets. Stusser repackaged the information again into a monthly "analysis letter" to suppliers who pay about $150 per month for his inside industry perspective.

What makes Daniel Stusser successful is that he has positioned himself as the central source of information by repackaging data from the $450 million vertical niche business known as the telecom management systems market.

## COMPUTER COUNTER

In 1964 Patrick McGovern's infopreneurial vision gave birth to the publishing and research and consulting empire, International Data Group (IDG). IDG is now a leader in repackaging and producing information service on information technology, meeting the information needs of more than 14 million people in over 30 countries.

More than 23 years ago, while working on assignment for an early trade publication, it struck McGovern that there was little information about who owned or leased computers, and how they were being used. McGovern saw the need for a computer installation census and for market trend analyses and projections based on this information.

From this early data gathering service, McGovern founded International Data Group and its market research and consulting division, International Data Corporation (IDC).

Today, IDC analyzes and tracks information on nearly 185,000 computer sites worldwide. From this database, IDC provides its clients with information services which track every major information technology market segment, highlighting major trends and developments. IDG services include written reports, unlimited telephone consultation, monthly newsletters, customized research, on-site consultation, and seminars and conferences.

Shortly after founding IDC, McGovern discovered another "information gap" beginning to emerge—computer systems managers needing to be kept up-to-date with the expanding array of computer hardware and software and their potential effects on their systems planning activity. *Computerworld* was created to meet this need, and today it is the industry's leading trade publication.

*Computerworld* is part of IDG's publishing division, IDG Communications. The division's worldwide staff of more than 490 editors and journalists contribute to an international news network which produces more than 90 publications around the globe including *PC World, Macworld, InfoWorld, Network World, Digital News,* and *Federal Computer Week* in the U.S. and *China Computerworld, Computerwoche* in Germany, *Computerworld Japan,* and *Le Mond Informatique* in France.

IDG Communications also negotiated the first joint venture publishing agreements in Hungary, the People's Republic of China, and most recently in the Soviet Union.

For infopreneur Pat McGovern, repackaging information is not an end in itself. He is simply meeting people's need for new and better information.


# REPACKAGING INFORMATION

Repackaging information starts by identifying the five different forms of information: voice, data, text, images, and pictures. Currently, each form of information is experiencing a radical reconstruction.

## Voice

Infopreneurs at Carnegie-Mellon University's Center for Machine Translation have designed a system prototype that converts speech into text. Soon, an American dialing a telephone number in France will not have to worry whether or not the person on the other end of the line is bilingual. A computer system hooked into the phone system instantly translates both ends of the conversation into the other's native tongue. This prototype system converts speech sounds into text, analyzes the context of the words, produces a translated text, then turns the text back into speech.

InfoPlus, a Boston electronic-publishing firm, also reconstructs voice through "talking ads." Its Yellow Pages Plus lets callers punch a code to hear recorded messages about a service or product offered. This reconstructed information combines the practicality of a directory with the packaging of a commercial.

Although the telephone has been around for more than a century, only recently has voice reconstruction occurred from 33,000 feet in the air. The infopreneur who started MCI Communications recently introduced Airfone, a service that puts public telephones on commercial airlines. With almost a million people a day in the sky, about one-third are placing calls since Airfone has been installed. Projections of 100 million calls a year from airplanes will generate at least $750 million in annual revenues.

Back on earth, another infopreneur was visiting a client when he spotted a trash bin full of letters and memos. Realizing that each piece of paper had cost his client about $8.00, he created a solution to this waste—a new industry called voice messaging. By dialing a special number, callers leave digitally recorded messages which can be retrieved by the recipient at any time. The advantages to reconstructing voice by means of voice messaging are that communication takes place just once, time zones become irrelevant, and the only equipment the caller needs is a telephone.

Soap Line, Inc. also reconstructs voice information by offering three tape recorded updates of soap operas at any time day or night. The soaps, which appear on the three television networks, are accompanied by a wide variety of local advertisements. This information service requires an automatic answering machine that can receive 12,000 calls a day, and plenty of publicity to succeed.

Voice reconstruction ideas can occur at any time, and under any circumstance. For example, when an infopreneur was parked at a red light and a carload of teenagers pulled up alongside his car, the radio station he was listening to switched to the one they were listening to. Confused by the technical aberration, he later learned that that radios not only receive signals, but also transmit. This infopreneur created a device that tells him what people listen to on their car radios.

He now sits in his parked car near intersections gathering information from car radios of passersby. He records:

- What station riders are listening to.
- The make and year of the car.
- The time of day and location.

He repackages this compiled information into a report and sells it to radio station owners and advertisers for between $850 and $2500.

## Data

Creating words is a hobby for some people, but creating names for products and companies is a business for others. One infopreneur makes his living by creating names for companies and products and charges up to $35,000 to reconstruct data that form unique names. This infopreneur designed the name Compaq which suggests small, integral computers. Compaq went on to become one of the fastest growing computer companies in history.

When a client requests a name, his company, NameLab, often creates "attributive nouns" which are accepted by consumers as a quality of the product. NameLab starts with a 3-hour introductory meeting with clients to agree on a ranked list of messages to be expressed in that chosen name. By reconstructing about 150 relatively sensible word combinations, this infopreneur pulls the 20 strongest candidates. The ultimate name is often a new expression that seems like a real word. Once the client chooses a name, pays the ownership fee, and has its legal eligibility determined, the reconstructed name is then widely proclaimed by the company.

One infopreneur began to reconstruct data through codes and ciphers. He eventually built a product around them. His *Decipher Puzzle* is a combination of puzzle and cipher which offers a $100,000 prize if it can be solved. More than 150,000 units were sold in its first year, grossing nearly two million dollars. Yet no one has successfully reconstructed the data to solve the problem and claim the prize.

Infopreneurs can reconstruct any type of data to create value. Recently three Dartmouth College juniors gathered 1300 terms associated with the arms race and created a book called, *Coming to Terms with Nuclear War: An A–Z Guide to Nuclear Weapons Technology.* This is the first comprehensive, nonbiased dictionary dedicated to the language of nuclear war. Repackaging information about nuclear terms started while one of the infopreneurs was reading an article on the arms race. He encountered several words he did not grasp and was unable to find satisfactory definitions in reference books. During his internship at the United Nations Institute for Disarmament Research, he compiled a master list of words and had two friends help in defining them.

As the old baseball park saying goes, "Get your program here" now has a new meaning in the dugout of the New York Mets where its infopreneurial manager relies on experience, instincts, and a personal computer to repackage data. The performances of athletes are programmed into the computer and the raw data is reconstructed to link the tangible aspects of the game. This manager no longer depends on baseball folklore or personal knowledge. His computer can reconstruct data to show histories of hitters versus pitchers, the best batting line-ups, and the most effective pitching rotations. Repackaged data also help his baseball scouts track thousands of professional and amateur ballplayers throughout the year. At draft time, the computer sorts out the players still available as 26 teams make 40 draft choices each.

With the assistance of repackaged data, this manager led the New York Mets farm team to two penants and guided the major league team to victory in the 1986 World Series.

Finally, on October 19, 1987, as investors frantically sold off huge blocks of stock to establish the largest loss on Wall Street in its 103-year history, infopreneurs at Wall Street Games were also busy selling and buying. A former stockbroker set up a game that lets the faint-hearted or noninvestor try a hand at investing a hypothetical $100,000 in any of 5000 actual stocks.

For a membership fee of $100 (in real money) the computer system simulates the trading of stocks. Each player is allowed up to 50 free calls a year, receives monthly statements, and can be ranked against the Dow and other players.

## Text

Reconstructing text occured when one of the first electronic journalists working in an interactive format wrote the book *Chronicle, The Human Side of AIDS*. The book was completed through on-line teleconferencing. The interactive nature of his work currently helps health care professionals treat patients by providing an exchange of information and new insights. This infopreneur repackaged his text on AIDS as participants provided him with leads and expertise.

In Salt Lake City, a revolutionary text service allows home computers to restructure a 50-page magazine called *Teletext-5* any time of the day or night. Unlike conventional bulletin board systems, which usually offer little more than a central message base and public domain software, *Teletext-5* repackages information from 17 different services, including news, weather, sports, and classified ads. Up to 12 users can tie into the system at any time without the need of a password to access the text.

As the dental insurance industry has become inundated with carriers, coverages, exclusions, deductibles, and limitations, two women infopreneurs have reconstructed its information to improve the dentist's ability to collect payment. Dental Insurance Services, Inc. provides information about employers and their insurance coverages to help anticipate the needs of the insurance carriers and provide patients with information about coverages.

## Images

The fourth type of information, images, has experienced great breakthroughs in reconstruction. One example is biometrics, which repackages biological characteristics such as fingerprints. Military bases use biometrics to screen admissions; banks use it to verify identification of its customers; fake identification cardholders can now be spotted instantly by the process.

Just in the security business, sales projections of biometric devices total $100 million by 1990. Scanning fingerprint images occurs when a person places a finger in a slot on a scanning machine. Within a few seconds a microprocessor translates the print into digital codes and matches it against codes stored in the computer's memory.

Another approach to reconstructing images is known as "fingerprints on a chip." An infopreneur built an inexpensive way, through digitized images, to put fingerprints inside credit card-sized identification cards. An integrated circuit inside the card contains the owner's digitized fingerprint images. When the card is slipped into a terminal and the person places a finger onto a glass plate, the machine scans the finger and compares the image with the data in the card When they match, access to the computer, building, or bank account is granted.

## Pictures

One perceptive infopreneur created a personal archive service based on the understanding that everyone's life is interesting and important. By videotaping conversations, loved ones can recount significant events, thoughts, and feelings so people can better understand themselves and their heritage. The service reconstructs information on videotape through its many interview options such as Christmas traditions, your early years, advice to children, your living will, your work, a typical day, America today, religious beliefs, your marriage, having a baby, what you are like, favorite music, literature, art, and much more. The videotaped history service allows participants to tell their own story in their own words.

Finally, pictures have been reconstructed by phone since the 1964 New York World's Fair. Little progress was made in the two decades following picturephone's introduction. However, two infopreneurs have recently designed a picturephone that manipulates incoming and outgoing visual data across phone lines.

The past limitations of the picturephone, technology and cost, have recently been minimized. The technological solution, repackaging the picture based on the changes in motion made from one frame to the next, means fewer details are sent over the lines. Transmitting smaller amounts of data keeps the quality of the overall picture high while costs stay low. The market has also shown a new readiness to embrace the new technology. When the cost of an industrial sales call exceeded $215 in 1985, the cost-efficiency of the picturephone became a reality.

## HOW TO RECONSTRUCT INFORMATION

Infopreneurs who reconstruct information tend to challenge prevailing views of how information should function. They solve problems as information is recombined and restructured. Quite often infopreneurs cannot predict what the final product of their repackaged voice, data, text, images, or pictures will be.

Infopreneurs require broad goals, specific objectives, and flexible strategies to provide a framework within which to repackage information. To build such a framework infopreneurs:

- *Assess resources.* Begin with a long, hard look at the myriad of sources for opportunities. Look for unrelated but relatable information.

- *Combine ideas.* Use the assessed resources to develop new ideas or create new relationships from among your information.
- *Test the ideas.* Today's risk takers become tommorrow's leaders. Adopt a risk-taking attitude with your new information ideas. Let an idea build its own momentum as you share it with other creative and risk-taking infopreneurs.
- *Take it to market.* Once your repackaged information has been tested, gain a market orientation from your customers. Develop a strong understanding of how you are providing a solution to an information problem in the market.
- *Repackage it.* Maintain flexibility and be prepared to modify the information's structure. Rarely will you hit a home run in your first time at bat with the repackaged information.
- *Focus on a single application.* The infopreneur with grand visions to revolutionize industries is unlikely to succeed. One common theme can be isolated from among the successes: When infopreneurs repackage information, their final products are simple and focused. Confusion is avoided because their products are directed toward specific and carefully designed applications.
- *Get there first.* Establish a long-term vision for your repackaged information, but be sure you get it to market before anyone else can duplicate or recreate it.

By following these steps, you can discover how to easily repackage information and turn data into dollars.

# 7

# PROVIDE
# AROUND-THE-CLOCK
# DELIVERY OF INFORMATION

A century ago, the Industrial Revolution helped companies achieve greater efficiency by substituting heavy machinery for human labor. Information, however, was still generated by people. During today's Information Revolution, computers substitute for human effort to process information at all hours.

Infopreneurs deliver information 24 hours a day to differentiate products and enhance services in the marketplace. Around-the-clock delivery of information offers several benefits for organizations in a competitive environment:

117

- It changes an organization's image in the marketplace.
- It creates a competitive advantage.
- It spawns new business opportunities.

The growth of nonstop information delivery is due to the fact that information impacts all corporate activities and reshapes consumer behavior. Information takes on a value-added quality once it becomes available any time of the day or night.

Information technology lets people dial one phone number and receive information about any product or service, at any time, from anywhere in the world. This dynamic forces companies to reexamine their information distribution policies, standardize methods of information delivery, and design the best ways to meet the around-the-clock work schedules and impulsive buying habits of the American consumer.

The Newsletter Association of America recently reported that businesses using 24-hour toll-free phone numbers receive 25 percent of their calls between 6 P.M. and 9 P.M.—after traditional working hours are completed. Around-the-clock delivery of information captures an entire market of buyers who want to control the time and place of their information deliveries.

Information technology can standardize any type of information for distribution on a 24-hour basis. For example, an accounting firm integrated a system to help people weigh the impact of recent tax reform on their tax returns—at any hour. People start with their previous year's tax form in front of them, then place a call from any Touch Tone phone. A synthesized computer voice answers and gives instructions. Callers punch their tax data into the accounting firm's computer via their own telephone key pad. The system provides valuable information for clients, prospective clients, or interested callers at any time without human attendant.

Another example of around-the-clock information delivery was designed by infopreneurs at Boise State University. Students with personal computers, telephone modems, and a charge card can order from the store's inventory of 1500 textbooks and 8000 general interest books 24 hours a day, seven days a week. Also available on the same basis are computer supplies, clothing, or other school items.

Delivery of information without time constraints has also become a major focus of divisions within the corporation:

- *Promotion*—uses toll-free 800 numbers and 900 numbers to provide instruction and data to order a product or request service information.
- *Advertising*—taps the potential of interactive information services.
- *Sales*—uses telemarketing to overcome the high cost of sales calls and time limitations of the field staff.
- *Research*—gains instant access to consumer attitudes through Touch Tone telephone responses.
- *Services*—access remote servicing of equipment such as on-line computer diagnostics in new model cars.
- *Products*—integrate computer-aided design and manufacturing to reduce design time and improve products.
- *Distribution*—utilizes on-line data systems for procurement of parts from around the world.
- *Information systems*—monitor consumer buying habits through direct ordering, electronic surveys, and on-site electronic coupons.
- *Logistics*—reduce costs and inventories through automated warehouses and order processing.
- *Human resource management*—provides appropriate staffing for periods of work through automated personnel scheduling.

As the Information Revolution sweeps through the economy, no company will escape its effects. Infopreneurs, providing access to information on demand, are creating structural changes in the corporate world. Companies that recognize and respond to these changes will gain a competitive edge through around-the-clock delivery of information.

## AROUND-THE-CLOCK TRADING

Bernard Rome applied information technology to create the world's first totally electronic trading exchange. Rome, founder and president of a computer-telephone-credit card trading network called Teletrade, offers a significant break-through in the way coins are bought and sold. Teletrade brings together numismatists (buyers and sellers of coins) through a totally electronic exchange that does not require the use of a personal computer. A Touch Tone phone is the only require-ment for trading of coins at any hour.

Rome's background in computers prepared him to revolu-tionize the age-old practice of numismatics. Rome has inte-grated information technology into many of his past business ventures from the preceding 30 years. The Teletrade network does not employ a single coin trader but simply acts as an infor-mation middleman to bring together buyers and sellers of coins.

Teletrade centralizes information to eliminate the ineffi-ciencies of face-to-face trading. Through a 24-hour toll-free phone number subscribers enter a computer password and then punch a series of buttons on the phone pad to designate the coin that they wish to purchase or sell. A synthesized voice tells its lowest asking price and the highest bid on file. To main-tain consistency and credibility, only coins graded by the American Numismatic Association Certification Services can be traded over Teletrade. The ANACS has issued grading cer-tificates on more than 500,000 coins.

Membership in Teletrade is open to any coin dealer, collec-tor, investor, or other interested party in the trading network. For $20 a month and a 4 percent commission on the price of coins through the network, members can buy, sell, or trade coins via the phone-in system and receive them within two business days. Pick-up and delivery charges are split between the buyers and sellers.

Bernard Rome has taken information technology one step further. He has introduced a series of video coin auctions which is open only to Teletrade subscribers.

Prospective bidders purchase video cassette tapes spot-lighting up to 300 lots of various U.S. coins. Tapes are sent free to numismatists who have purchased coins from Teletrade over the previous year. On the tape each coin is rotated for an average of ten seconds to give a view of its strike, surface characteristics, and color.

The auction lasts seven hours, and prospects can obtain the most recent bid by dialing a toll-free number. Callers can enter a bid or proceed to another lot number.

Teletrade is the world's first totally electronic trading system to give subscribers the information they need when they want it. Bernard Rome has revolutionized the antiquated method of coin trading by the use of information technology. Teletrade's unique approach provides up-to-the-minute prices on the coins available. Fulfillment of numismatic needs are now just a phone call away any time of the day or night.

# AROUND-THE-CLOCK REAL ESTATE PRICES

In 1930, Rufus S. Lusk, Jr. began publishing real estate directories and statistical analyses of the Washington, D.C. metropolitan area. Today, 58 years later, Rufus S. Lusk and Son, Inc. produce over 60 publications a year ranging from weekly compilations of real estate sales and mortgage information to annual property maps in hard-copy and property assessment and ownership data in microfiche. In its newest venture Lusk invested $1 million to provide around-the-clock real estate information through a service called LUSKNET.

Subscribers tap into LUSKNET to find out:

- What type of property is selling where.
- Who is buying and selling.
- Price and mortgate information.

Lusk collects raw data from courthouses and city or county assessment offices, then organizes this data for easy reference through weekly guides, quarterly, semi-annual, and annual directories, and special studies. As part of the process, the inputted data are also prepared for on-line access by appraisers, brokers, agents, lenders, investors, and property managers any time, day or night.

Although LUSKNET does not provide any additional data for subscribers to Lusk's books, the computerized information offers new ways to organize and retrieve the data around-the-clock. The computer provides instant access to market figures and helps pinpoint new trends. LUSKNET saves time, improves the quality of market analysis, and provides the only comprehensive electronic real estate sales information for the entire Metropolitan Washington, D.C. area.

LUSKNET's primary market is current subscribers to the Lusk real estate publications. For those with in-house computers, Lusk offers a free trial before they buy. Prospective buyers receive one month of free service. When they subscribe to the service, Lusk gives them a second month free, which lets them learn to use the service cost-effectively. LUSKNET subscribers also receive a 60 percent price break if they already subscribe to Lusk's other publications.

With half of all real estate agents expected to own personal computers by 1990, Lusk weighed the risk of the investment into LUSKNET against the market potential for his service. He felt the return was worth the risk.

Individuals and organizations pay for 12 hours worth of computer on-line service in advance (one hour per month)— $288 ($24/hour) for subscribers and $720 ($60/hour) for non-subscribers. These hourly rates are further discounted by 50 percent between the hours of 6 P.M. and 8 A.M. on weekdays.

Lusk is firmly committed to electronic real estate information services but also sees a bright future for distributing data via other media, whether hard-copy or microfiche. Rufus S. Lusk, III, current president and grandson of the founder, states that the key to the information business is to distribute data the subscribers truly need in a form that is most appropriate to their purposes.

## AROUND-THE-CLOCK TEACHING

In Brooklyn, New York, Rabbi Eli Teitelbaum makes the wisdom of the past more accessible through the use of information technology and his Torah Communications Network. In 1982, two anonymous donors made a combined gift of $75,000 to launch a nonprofit project called Dial-a-Daf (Daf is Hebrew for "page").

By dialing a personal number that can be accessed any time without getting a busy signal, subscribers listen to taped lectures in Hebrew or English of the Talmud—the legal tradition of Judaism. Day or night, lectures start promptly on the hour, except on such occasions as the Sabbath and the High Holy Days, when Jewish law forbids using the telephone. At the pace of a page a day, a thorough teaching of the Talmud is accomplished in seven years.

One advantage of the service is that subscribers can choose when and how much to listen to at a sitting. If a mother can hear only the first half of the tape in the morning, she can call back in the afternoon at half past the hour and pick up the rest of the lecture. The peak hours for the service are from 6 A.M. to 8 A.M., noon to 2 P.M., and 8 P.M. to midnight. If a subscriber misses a day, the tape can be purchased for $1.00. The original system handled 300 callers an hour.

By 1987, the network had grown into an international organization with services available around the globe. Branches and tape libraries are now located in 23 cities throughout the United States, Canada, England, and Israel. It has since introduced two new projects, Dial-a-Shiur and Mishnah-on-the-Phone. These programs make available a variety of Torah lectures on topics other than the Talmud.

In New York alone, the network has attracted more than 3000 subscribers which include lawyers, business executives, and doctors. Membership involves a $36 initial fee and $6.00 per month thereafter. As the program's reputation grows, infopreneur Teitelbaum receives an influx of tapes from authorities who, in effect, are auditioning for a place on the program. The annual budget is now more than $250,000 with the current system handling about 600 callers per hour.

Most subscribers use speaker phones so that listening may be done in groups, over lunch, or in the evenings. The application of this around-the-clock information service has expanded into several area hospitals allowing patients to hear the tapes at any time.

Torah Communication Network has enriched Jewish culture and lifestyle by providing motivated listeners with teachings of the Torah and the Talmud. Information is provided to subscribers around-the-clock from a New York rabbi/infopreneur. This innovative system of information delivery helps challenge the intellectual and spiritual needs of its subscribers.


## ON-LINE CUSTOMER INFORMATION

In 1981, with interest rates floating near 21 percent, Fielding Yost went to a bank and asked for a loan to finance his service bureau called Saturn. Yost wanted to offer the direct mail and data processing industries a first: 24-hour access to processed information about their customers.

In just seven years Saturn generated billings of $7 million. Yost's service targets nonprofit organizations with customer files of at least 50,000 names. The value of Yost's around-the-clock information is that product, service, or information requests can be fulfilled in a timely manner, producing customer satisfaction in the marketplace.

As the end of the century approaches, nonprofit organizations will attempt some radical changes because of the need to deliver information on demand. Through information management systems, what used to take months to accomplish in the 1960s, took just weeks to accomplish in the 1970s. With advances in computer hardware and software, what took weeks to do in the 1970s took only days in the 1980s. Finally, what took only days, Saturn is now accomplishing within hours, even instantly for the 1990s. To understand and achieve information's full potential, Yost provides customers with his in-house computer system because it meets the current demands of the marketplace.

The 1990s, era of the on-line interactive environment, will bring radical changes to the way Yost's nonprofit clients think and act. Faster information allows them to identify changes in the market, their organizations, or services, as well as instantly:

- Reactivate recently lapsed supporters.
- Acknowledge new members.
- Cross-sell to recent buyers.
- Upgrade levels of subscribers.

- Thank donors for their gifts.
- Respond to complaints or errors.

And much much more.

As one of the first service bureaus to offer real-time interactive information around-the-clock, Saturn's network architecture and software puts information in the hands of the end-user when they want it. Nonprofit organizations no longer need in-house computers or the staff to manage them. The information clients enter from remote sites is instantly updated by Saturn.

Saturn became a nationwide service bureau with clients in 35 states because infopreneur Fielding Yost used information technology to meet his clients' needs for up-to-the-minute information immediately available. This breakthrough provides a way for nonprofit organizations to succeed in the Information Age.

# RESTAURANT INFORMATION SERVICE

Infopreneur Bruce Kallenberg created the New York Restaurant Hot Line as a way to help people select restaurants that suit their tastes and budgets, 24 hours a day.

When his New York Restaurant Hot Line began, Kallenberg had more than 150 participating restaurants. Although the service offers free consumer-oriented information to callers, the Hot Line receives $2 from restaurants each time a reservation is placed through it. If, however, the caller receives a Hot Line recommendation but books a reservation without using the Restaurant Hot Line's reservation service, the Hot Line does not collect its $2 fee from the restaurant.

Restaurant recordings are designed from the restaurant's own press releases, published ads, and from data gathered during personal visits by Kallenberg and his staff. Kallenberg's infopreneurial venture currently divides Manhattan into four sections with separate phone numbers for the East and West Sides above and below 59th Street.

When people call, a recorded message asks callers about the kind of food, price range, and location they prefer. In order to respond, callers must punch designated restaurant numbers from a Touch Tone telephone. A computer matches their requests with tape recorded messages about the restaurants. The computer then proceeds to reserve a table for callers. When callers punch in a three-digit code, the computer directly connects them to the desired restaurant.

Many callers wanting a table in the best restaurants in New York and at the last minute, often stand a better chance when going through the New York Restaurant Hot Line, even where tables are difficult to secure on short notice.

The New York Restaurant Hot Line is an information service that meets the needs of unsure restaurant goers. Besides the fact that the service costs the consumer nothing to use, it is available any time day or night. It takes a receptive infopreneur like Bruce Kallenberg to pioneer a new form of 24-hour-a-day advertising.

## PROVIDING AROUND-THE-CLOCK DELIVERY OF INFORMATION

Information has become America's biggest business. The information sector of the American economy, which ranked below agriculture, manufacturing, and services back in 1910, led all categories in 1980. Information processing and delivery now accounts for half of all American workforce activities. Through the end of the century, the greatest capital expenditures will occur in the information sector, not necessarily to create new data, rather to provide its delivery around the clock. While the cost of information storage and manipulation has dropped, the opportunities for information transmittal have expanded.

## INFRASTRUCTURE FOR INFORMATION DELIVERY

The value of time-sensitive information was appreciated by Nathan Rothschild, who became wealthy through learning the outcome of the Battle of Waterloo before members of the London Stock Exchange.

Rothschild designed an elaborate communications infrastructure which consisted of carrier pigeons, semaphores, packet boats, and couriers on horseback. The ability to gather and disseminate critical information gave Rothschild an edge in the financial marketplace.

In today's world of around-the-clock information delivery, infopreneurs have created applications for consumers as well as corporations. The infrastructure that provides unrestricted access to information is currently in place and includes:

- *Library information.* Through on-line networks and PCs infopreneurs can access hundreds of library data bases from the convenience of their living rooms.
- *Call forwarding from home.* Infopreneurs never need to miss important phone calls again because of technological breakthroughs which allows telephone calls to be forwarded to other locations.
- *Recorded messages in central locations.* Electronic mail provides a "mail box for voices" which allows callers to leave messages and obtain responses at any time.
- *Shopping information via television and telephone.* Home shopping clubs and networks let infopreneurs shop any time of the day or night without leaving home.
- *Financial information.* Infopreneurs can access stock and bond information around-the-clock by telephone.
- *Home management systems.* Infopreneurs can program appliances from their coffee pots to their jacuzzis through a Touch Tone phone from anywhere in the world at any time.
- *Automated messaging.* Infopreneurs can send messages automatically through alert systems. The opening and closing of a refrigerator can be monitored to keep tabs on independent senior citizens.
- *Newspaper and magazine transmittal.* Infopreneurs can receive newspapers and magazines electronically on their own time schedules through home computers.
- *Offsite work.* Telecommuters are people who work from home or satellite offices. Information technology lets

them obtain and submit work around-the-clock from a home computer via modem.

Among the many applications of 24-hour information delivery, these two may be the most significant for infopreneurs in the Information Age:

- *Televoting.* Local leaders, elected to represent the people, need to know how their constituents feel about issues. Televoting gives people a convenient way to be involved in community decisions or offer a direct voice to their representatives. Computerized telephone systems allow voters to "dial in" their votes.
- *Job Hotline.* Chief executives from local companies can form a repository of qualified, yet recently laid-off employees. The computerized list of laid-off workers, organized by job description, can be made available to other business owners through a toll-free phone number or on-line computer network at any hour.

# FRAMEWORK FOR DESIGNING AN AROUND-THE-CLOCK INFORMATION DELIVERY SYSTEM

Around-the-clock information delivery can become a complex and expensive undertaking. Infopreneurs are often overwhelmed by the technologies and processes required to deliver information on a 24-hour basis. The following phases provide a structure for the revolutionary task of distributing information without time constraints:

### PHASE I:   Commitment to Nonstop Information Delivery

*Select a fact-finding task force.*
1. Notify members
2. Assign responsibilities to schedule and monitor
3. Explore alternative approaches to information delivery

*Prepare a pilot program of the best alternative.*
1. Set the start date

2. Determine the measurement criteria
3. Establish milestones and benchmarks
   - Tasks
   - Responsibilities
   - Deadlines

### Prepare a budget.
1. Determine financial needs
2. Establish a cash flow timeline

## PHASE II: Full Implementation Design

### Acquire facilities.
1. Work space
2. Utilities
3. Furnishings

### Order equipment hardware and software.
1. Data and word processing
2. Telecommunications
3. Support equipment

### Design a business communications plan.
1. Customer segments
2. Marketing communications
3. Support and reference materials

### Establish interface structures.
1. Identify critical interfaces among departments
2. Design interface procedures

### Determine information-delivery productivity requirements.
1. Identify information content and format
2. Establish methods for information delivery
3. Design a procedures manual
4. Establish measurement criteria and record keeping

## PHASE III: Plan Staffing, Training, and Education

### Establish job descriptions.
1. Information manager
2. Supervisor
3. Specialists
4. Support staff

*Design staff recruitment and selection processes.*
1. Establish selection criteria
2. Announce positions
3. Schedule interviews
4. Select and announce staff

*Arrange for training.*
1. Establish content
2. Arrange training sites
3. Complete program

## PHASE IV: Other Considerations for Information Delivery

*Determine information capacity.*
1. Examine current and future applications
2. Evaluate current and emerging technologies
3. Explore deterrents to successful implementation

*Establish a corporate information policy.*
1. Link information delivery to the corporate mission
2. Examine the information flow throughout entire company
3. Determine costs and payback period

Three benchmarks of productivity in around-the-clock delivery of information include: customer identification, personnel disintermediation, and market penetration. Your program will succeed when the following events occur simultaneously:

- Critical information about customers (name, address, and phone number) is captured;
- Personnel resources and overhead expenses are reduced or eliminated;
- Access to current and untapped markets suddenly becomes available.

## WHERE TO START

Implementation of around-the-clock information delivery requires a special attention to detail. To succeed, infopreneurs must:

1. Use company orientations to make sure the program is understood by all involved.
2. Facilitate the process by working within existing corporate structures.
3. Involve the users in the change so that they have a stake in its success.
4. Get the staff's views on the requirements of the system.
5. Build on success by repeating it. If a system works for one department, let them sell the application to another.
6. Introduce only one new information system at a time. Allow for the assimilation of the technology and application.
7. Point out to the staff how they personally benefit from the new information delivery system.
8. Find a program champion—someone who likes the new idea and will make sure it succeeds.

## THE TWENTY-FIRST CENTURY

A 24-hour information service can be accomplished cost-effectively through the creative application of today's information technology. Around-the-clock delivery of information will bring about the greatest changes in work patterns since factories displaced the farmer. By the end of the century, infopreneurs will deliver most of the information in society around-the-clock as they turn data into dollars.

Information technology alone cannot advance the Information Revolution. Infopreneurs creatively applying the technology will be the cornerstone of progress into the next century. In many instances, an old technology applied in a new way by a creative infopreneur brings dramatic results.

The biggest breakthroughs by infopreneurs may be in providing information around-the-clock. In this case, information actually takes on new functions as the information becomes as easy to access as electricity through a light switch. The following parameters should help infopreneurs who want to provide information at anytime:

- Establish a philosophy that defines useful information.
- Set measurement criteria for the use of that information.
- Identify all intended uses for the information.
- Determine key interfaces to monitor the flow of information.
- Manage the information to eliminate duplication.
- Provide feedback controls to insure information performance.

Once these guidelines are in place, the role of information can be determined by the infopreneur. Although a record number of new jobs has been created in recent years, 24-hour delivery of information may bring on significant job displacement in the long term.

Just as the Industrial Revolution displaced farmers into the manufacturing sector, the Information Revolution has displaced blue collar workers of the manufacturing sector into the "thinking business" of the service sector. If the trends toward global wage leveling and automated factories continue, the U.S. manufacturing sector will shrink by nearly 90 percent in less than two decades. It will be up to the service sector to absorb these 22 million displaced workers.

This scenario paints the picture of a limited number of automated factories producing vast quantities of quality products, while millions of people go without work. As this pool of unemployed workers retools with today's information technology, they can provide information at all hours to increase manufacturing productivity and improve service quality.

## NEW PATHWAYS TO PRODUCTIVITY

With the advent of information 24 hours a day, it is possible to run a continuous flow of information through computers and telephones by making simple programming adjustments. Flexible programs can process an idea into marketable information in a matter of hours rather than in months, as in the past. With today's information and communication technology breakthroughs, few barriers prevent delivering information around-the-clock.

When contemplating how to provide your information at any time day or night follow these steps before you invest:

1. Step back from your venture to gain a new sense of objectivity.
2. Study the successes of other infopreneurs providing 24-hour information.
3. Isolate market niches for information not currently offered day and night.
4. Attend trade shows and conventions to obtain the most recent examples about information movement technologies.
5. Consider how a series of information delivery steps can be combined into a single process.
6. Apply fresh options for delivering new types of information around-the-clock within the context of expensive energy and labor.

These steps were obviously considered by an Oregon music company that offered a new kind of piano lesson, "a mini-lesson," by phone, 24 hours a day. Keyboard Workshop offers Dial-A-Piano-Lesson, that features a new playing tip every week. Each three-minute recorded lesson features some piano technique or style to improve one's playing.

The lesson is free to the caller, except for the cost of the call. Once the lesson is completed, a recorded voice comes on the line and offers a free transcript of the lesson and a catalog of the musical products offered by the music store. The benefit, of course, is that a local store has achieved national exposure, within its speciality, 24 hours a day, through the creative application of information technology.

## DETERMINING THE COST AND VALUE OF INFORMATION

The ability to provide information around-the-clock requires tight controls over the cost to generate and deliver this information. Answering these questions will help ensure that the 24-hour information value is greater than the cost to generate and deliver it:

- If this information becomes available, what problems can be solved, decisions made, or objectives achieved?
- What competitive advantage is created when the problems are solved, decisions made, or objectives achieved?
- What are the downside risks if this information does not become available?
- What are the ways the information can be delivered day or night?
- What other facets of the organization are benefited by around-the-clock delivery of information.

The cost of information delivered takes into account the total amount of resources required to create and deliver the information. To account for the cost of information, consider your information's three cost centers: labor, material, and overhead. Within these cost centers, the following recommendations will help control and reduce the costs of your information system:

- Either hire a third-party equipment maintenance firm to service your entire information system, or buy your information system from one firm who can service it completely.
- Locate the most respected suppliers in your area and get their opinions about how to reduce your costs.
- Consider the responsiveness and attention to detail of local third party service firms over national manufacturers or vendors.
- Reconsider your need for four-hour service when your back-up system is functioning.
- Utilize your service instruction manual and service hotlines to remedy equipment problems yourself.
- Remove the problem piece of equipment yourself and take it to a service firm to eliminate the cost of on-site service.
- Use information technology only as it is designed to be applied and eliminate any unnecessary uses.

- Establish a maintenance schedule and stick to it to eliminate costly repairs.
- Become a comparison shopper of service contracts to keep costs down and service up.

The challenge to become profitable with all-hour delivery of information requires the infopreneur not to just quantify the information, but to account for it—just as any other asset on the balance sheet. The first step is to define information's role in the organization.

The priorities attached to the various forms of information must be defined and managed. Around-the-clock information will then be considered a corporate asset, which makes it inherently more valuable. And what is valuable is generally better protected and secured.

One way to determine information's value is through a cost-based valuation, similar to calculating the cost of manufacturing a product. With this method, not only do you calculate the cost of accumulating and storing the information, but you also take into account the depreciation of the aging data.

A second method for determining information's value is through an appraisal-based valuation, similar to the real estate industry. In this case, the infopreneur calculates the current market value of the information, its ability to produce income, and the cost to replace the information.

When engaging a plan to provide information day or night, ask yourself three simple questions:

1. How much does the information cost to deliver?
2. How much revenue will the information generate relative to its cost?
3. What are the options for delivering more information at a lower cost?

In the broadest sense, the ability to process information and deliver it to the market around-the-clock, is an infopreneur's most valuable asset. It is this capability that allows the infopreneur to turn data into dollars.

# 8

# INTEGRATE THE
# INFORMATION TRIANGLE

One of the most important dynamics to the success of infopreneurs is the *Information Triangle*, which integrates computer—telephone—electronic funds transfer technologies to provide immediate payment for information generated and delivered.

The Information Triangle has emerged suddenly and without warning due to the widespread use of computers, telephones, and credit cards. Today among American adults, 98 percent own a telephone, 50 percent utilize one or more credit cards, and 20 percent own computers.

When the Information Triangle is designed into any organization or infopreneurial venture it can:

- Improve market penetration.
- Increase the value of information.
- Differentiate a service or product through reduced cost and faster delivery.

Yet the most important benefit of the Information Triangle is that it produces immediate cash flow.

The Information Triangle has revolutionized the way information and money are exchanged. By 1999 half of all financial transactions will be conducted through some form of electronic funds exchange. Electronic payment provides infopreneurs with immediate payment for the information they generate. This transaction can be as simple as taking a credit card number over the phone or having the phone company serve as bill collector.

The emergence of the Information Triangle can be traced back to the technological breakthroughs of the telephone, computer, and credit card, along with the shifting ratio of values among energy, labor, and capital, resulting from OPEC's oil embargo. Within the Information Triangle, telecommunications reduces excessive energy consumption from transportation, the value of labor is lowered as computerized automation outperforms people at less cost, and money is moved around the world in less than a second through electronic funds transfer.

Information technology and the shifting values among labor, energy, and capital has created a new economic model and opened the way for infopreneurs to produce better information and greater profits. The Information Triangle helps extend the capabilities of business in the same way the telescope extends the vision of the eye—offering business a view of its next productivity breakthrough.

Since the advent of automation in the late 1950s, manufacturing productivity increased 100 percent in less than 30 years. The Information Triangle takes automation one step further by reducing intermediary costs associated with producing and delivering information, services, and products. As the Information Triangle absorbs traditional business functions it is establishing new business models:

- *Politics.* In a recent Congressional campaign, one candidate integrated the Information Triangle to contact 40,000 registered Democrats in his Congressional District. Using a computer program, six phone lines, and a leased computer, the candidate overcame his opponent's mass mailings and radio advertisements. The computer/telephone operation was set up in a basement where the computer dialed telephone numbers from 9 A.M. until 9 P.M. Mondays through Fridays. On Saturdays the calling started at 11:30 A.M. and on Sundays from 1 P.M. until 8 P.M. The computer invited people to respond by Touch Tone phone. They could press "1" for literature and "2" to talk with a volunteer or make a donation immediately by phone with a credit card. The system, referred to as an "electronic town crier," told people where the candidate stood on issues and conducted constituent surveys.
- *Entertainment.* Following the success of Trivial Pursuit, the founder of The Source Telecomputing Company integrated the Information Triangle to introduce Prize Line Communications, an at-home telephone game arcade. A data base of more than 10,000 trivia questions is stored and anyone with a Touch Tone phone and credit card can play. Participants call a toll-free number and the computer assigns them a code. A computer-activated voice asks callers trivia questions. Answers are punched in on a key pad from the Touch Tone phone. It is the Information Triangle (computer-generated questions, a telephone conduit, and the electronic transfer of funds) that lets people pay as they play. Prearranged credit through direct phone billing or credit cards allows players to tap into the data base of questions. More than 2000 callers each month spend between $1.00 and $5.00 per game in Prize Line's trivia venture.
- *Retailing.* Comp-U-Card International is a computerized shopping service which offers the benefits of computerized shopping to people without computers—the next major revolution in retailing. Its current data bank lists more than 60,000 items at discounts up to 40 percent off

## INTEGRATE THE INFORMATION TRIANGLE

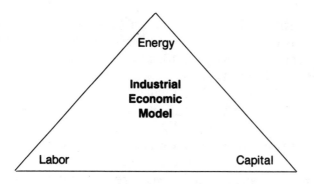

Energy

**Industrial
Economic
Model**

Labor                    Capital

INDUSTRIAL AGE

- - - - - - - - - - - - - - - - - - - - - - - - - - - - - - - - -

INFORMATION AGE

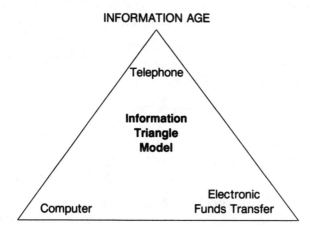

Telephone

**Information
Triangle
Model**

Computer

Electronic
Funds Transfer

the suggested retail price. Shoppers call a toll-free line, give the model number of the item desired, and are quoted a price that includes tax and delivery. The information can be used for comparison shopping—which is what about 60 percent of its members do, or to place an order. Comp-U-Card International, the nation's first and largest electronic shopping service, makes electronic shopping available to more than four million consumers nationwide through its Information Triangle. Customers simply call toll-free to tap the data base, then buy over the phone with their credit cards.

- *Television.* Hot Rock, Inc. is a 24-hour telemarketing music store that integrates the Information Triangle to offer convenience shopping for any record album, cassette, or video in print. Three Harvard infopreneurs launched Hot Rock, which generated sales of more than $6 million in its first year. The venture targets suburbanite professionals between the ages of 21 and 35 with a credit card and very little time to shop for records. Hot Rock fulfills more than 500 orders each day from phone calls. Its toll-free number is advertised on MTV, reaching more than 13 million households. The ability to penetrate a receptive audience, capture impulsive buyers through credit card orders via a toll-free call, then manage large amounts of information through the computer demonstrates the power of the Information Triangle.

The Information Triangle facilitates immediate response from market niches without extra labor, overhead, or capital. It is revolutionizing business by:

- Providing unique ways to penetrate and exploit market niches.
- Facilitating competition on new levels.
- Integrating innovative distribution strategies.
- Expediting data and payments electronically.

At the heart of the Information Triangle is its ability to improve productivity and eliminate costly intermediaries. As information technology centralizes specialized services and decentralizes routine interactions, infopreneurs integrate the Information Triangle to rearrange the methods by which goods, services, and information are delivered worldwide.

## INSTANT ART APPRAISALS

The Information Triangle can transform a local business into an international success. Such is the case of Telepraisal.

To determine the value of a given work of art, Carol Prisant, a Roslyn, New York, art appraiser, had to research prices previously paid for the item or for similar items by the same artist. This information was often difficult to locate and quite out of date by the time it was printed. The lack of reliable art pricing information led Carol and her son, Barden, to gather price reports from art auction houses around the world. Barden fed the information into his computer, and together they started Telepraisal in 1982. Since then, Telepraisal has keypunched thousands of auction catalog listings to create a computer data base of 600,000 works by nearly 60,000 artists together with biographical information on 300,000 more artists.

After Barden designed the software program to manage the data, he advertised a toll-free telephone number in *The Boston Globe*. That first day Telepraisal serviced 40 inquiries. In their first year of business, the Prisants provided art histories over the telephone to more than 8000 customers which included art dealers, corporations, collectors, and museums.

To use Telepraisal's Information Triangle, clients simply call its toll-free phone number, then give the artist's name and a description of the art work to an appraiser. The appraiser calls up the price history on a computer screen and relays the information to the client. Payment is then made over the phone by credit card. Written confirmations are also available as part of the service.

Once the computer, telephone, and credit card were integrated into Telepraisal's business structure, the following benefits were accrued:

- A large data base became instantly accessible.
- A global business was created.
- Payment was received at the time the information was provided.

The success of Telepraisal is the result of integrating the Information Triangle to let a person call from anywhere in the world, and for $30 know the value of an art piece in a matter of minutes.

# INSTANT STOCK QUOTES

Infopreneur Wayne Lemley, at age 26, started U.S. Quotes to make stock quotations available to anyone with a Touch Tone telephone. From his efficiency apartment, Lemley built a computer and a computerized stock-quote service which was unique in the financial services marketplace.

Subscribers deposit $45 to open an account. They are charged 12 cents per minute for stock information during market hours or six cents per minute after hours.

Lemley brought his Information Triangle to Wall Street to eliminate information intermediaries for those requesting only stock quotes. Investors who call discount brokers for stock information are often put on hold after a price request, while full-service brokers often pressure investors to make trades.

Yet, with U.S. Quotes, there is no wait and no hassle. Subscribers dial the computer and punch in ticker symbols on any of 25,000 stocks. The computer gives subscribers instructions on how to obtain their desired market information, then deducts the charges electronically from the deposit until the account is depleted. Subscribers are notified by computer when they must make another deposit to keep access to the computer.

As a value-added service, the computer allows subscribers to record lists of stocks which eliminates punching them in each time the information is requested.

The two technologies currently providing stock quotes are digital broadcasting, which unscrambles stock information transmitted over unused portions of FM radio bands, and audiotext, which has subscribers push buttons on Touch Tone phones to indicate which quotes are desired with a computer's synthesized voice providing the latest prices.

Lemley's audiotext quote service enlisted nearly 5000 subscribers (including complimentary trials) in its first year of business. Lemley was fresh out of graduate school when he seized the opportunity to integrate the Information Triangle. Lemley's service has only two requirements: the caller know the ticker symbol for the stock and that the call be made from a Touch Tone phone.

Recently other infopreneurs and corporations have entered

the stock quotation arena. The New York and American Stock Exchanges now offer up-to-the-second quotes. But what sets Lemley apart from his competitors is his ability to provide a better service at a lower cost. And his strategy to keep costs down and quality high—build his own computers.

## INSTANT MESSAGES

Today interactive voice services exceed $1 billion in annual revenue from among 400 "976" programmers, 2500 sponsored services, and 80 voice message service bureaus. By 1991 the interactive voice services market will be a 4.1 billion dollar industry.

Infopreneur Dave Meade integrated the Information Triangle to sponsor three talk lines through his Pennsylvania company called Party Line USA. His information services target specific populations outside the Philadelphia area with 976-BLAB for teenagers, 976-TALK for single adults, and 976-CALL for professional people. The low overhead and no accounts receivable for "976" lines are the unique features which have accounted for the growing interest in such information services.

The 976 Dial-it services are positioned as a new information medium which competes with the broadcast media for participants and revenues. The 976 services have become a technological phenomenon in today's Information Revolution. New information services spring up every day including the latest celebrity gossip line, 976-TRUE, and the extraterrestrial updates, 976-UFOS. After the explosion of recorded jokes and sports scores, the 976 applications spread into the interactive realm. Dial-a-Wake-Up is the first call-in service that calls back. By dialing the special phone number from a Touch Tone phone, a caller can punch in the time and number for an automatic wake-up or reminder call.

In the case of Meade's 976 talk-lines, it is a take off of the old-fashioned telephone party line which has been recycled as one of the fads of the 1980s. Talk-lines can connect up to eight callers at a time who use them to make dates, tell jokes, or just become friends. A talk-line is only as good as its participants.

Charging anywhere from $1.50 to $2.50 for six minutes, Dave Meade gives callers the opportunity to meet and talk to others or just listen in. Participants often exchange personal phone numbers to pursue more intimate conversations at a later time. Meade advertises his information service in every high school and college newspaper in the Philadelphia area.

One benefit of the Dial-it service is that the phone company acts as the bill collector. Each time someone calls the information service, a charge is added to the caller's phone bill. The phone company turns over half of the revenue to the sponsor of the program and keeps the other half for themselves.

Dial-it came on the scene after an FCC ruling declared that the phone company could no longer control the information content distributed over the telephone.

A decade ago, the only information lines available were for time and weather. Today, hundreds of Dial-it numbers, all with the 976 prefix, are offered at costs from 20 cents to $2.00. Messages range from stock quotes to horoscopes, from party jokes to sports scores, and of course, sexual messages.

The secret to the success of Dial-it services is the Information Triangle. An infopreneur creates a message that the phone company transmits over its lines. The phone company tracks the activity by computer, bills the participants, collects the money, then pays the owner of the program.

Dial-it services may seem frivolous or merely entertaining, but they offer a glimpse into the future when large amounts of information will be delivered by phone.

The 976 Dial-it service has opened up new opportunities for infopreneurs to integrate the Information Triangle. From 2100 American cities, Dial-it services generated three billion calls to time and weather in the first year of deregulation. An additional 500 million calls were placed to other Dial-it services, such as Meade's Party Line USA. These calls also generate additional income for the restructured phone companies.

Even though many Dial-it messages vary in length, producers of information services can create added revenue by selling one or more commercials that run at the beginning or in the middle of the recorded message.

## INSTANT WAGERING

In an effort to boost declining attendance and broaden the market for horse racing, infopreneur Mary Calabrese established a telephone wagering system at The Meadows Racetrack in Washington, Pennsylvania. This is the first time the Information Triangle has been used in legalized gambling at the races.

Call-a-Bet, launched in April, 1983, allows telephone wagering—which is not considered off-track betting since all wagering takes place at the track. In its first year Call-a-Bet at The Meadows had over 2000 subscribers who contributed $1.5 million to the track's $62 million in wagering during the racing season. Call-a-Bet now produces an average of $50,000 per night in bets which adds nearly $12 million to the annual handle.

The problem of declining attendance and subsequent betting necessitated the integration of the Information Triangle for race track wagering. In 1976 The Meadows experienced a record handle of $76 million. Then just six years later, wagering dropped by nearly 20 percent to $62 million. Call-a-Bet was tested so racing fans could place bets from the convenience of their homes and rejuvenate horse track wagering.

Call-a-Bet wagering, restricted to Pennsylvania residents 18 years of age and up, begins when $50 is deposited in an account at the track. Subscribers are sent a plastic identification card imprinted with a four digit account number and a toll-free phone number. Subscribers also receive a security code name similar to personal identification numbers used by automated bank teller machines. The number, known only by the subscriber, is used to call up for a wager. When placing a bet, callers give their account numbers and code names. Bet amounts are fed into a computer by Call-a-Bet operators at the track. Phone calls are tape-recorded to eliminate any misunderstandings.

When the account is depleted another deposit is required. The computer automatically totals the winnings or losses, then adds or deducts that amount from the account. Such a breakthrough clearly demonstrates how the Information Triangle can transform any venture, even race track betting at The Meadows.

# PHONE WORDS

Infopreneur James Novack has a cure for "Phone Number Amnesia"—that nagging problem everyone faces when they cannot remember someone's phone number. He programmed his computer to create personalized phone numbers and integrated the Information Triangle to generate instant payment for his innovative information service. Novack started Panaventure's Letter Dial from his Los Angeles home to help people do more for less with their telephone numbers.

Rather than paying a premium to purchase an existing phone number, Novack figured there was a business sorting through the 2187 letter combinations of a customer's current phone number. If their current phone number could spell out a word or express an idea, the client would then have the opportunity to advertise its alpha translation and associate it with a product, person, or service.

Novack's Letter Dial runs a customer's business or residential phone number through its proprietary software and prints out a list of alpha translated possibilities. The charge for businesses is $25 and for private lines $15. Payment is made over the phone by credit card.

Novack often suggests testing other local exchanges to find the optimal local phone number. He charges another $25 for Letter Dial to run a batch of five available prefixes which may suggest a word or idea that can be finished off with the four remaining digits if the combination has not already been assigned. For one maker of tanning creams, Letter Dial came up with a prefix that could spell RUB. Novack then suggested RUB-IT-IN and RUB-IT-ON as phone numbers for the company.

Personalized telephone numbers have become the latest fad following the introduction of personalized license plates. Local phone companies started offering "vanity phone numbers" by giving a customer the choice of the last four digits. Rather than obtain a new phone number with a new exchange, Novack often helps customers find words from within their current phone numbers.

Pacific Bell Telephone Company predicts that by 1991 nearly one million of its customers will obtain personalized phone numbers. Once the phone company helps locate a number, residential customers are charged an initial set-up fee plus $1.50 per month while businesses pay a $38 one-time fee plus $3.00 per month.

Novack saw how he could do more for less by simply taking a person's existing phone number then match it with the letters on the dial. More often than not, his nine-page computer printout generates a clever and memorable word.

Novack's innovative use of the Information Triangle may someday solve the problem of "Phone Number Amnesia" and result in people's saying, "Here's my *phone word.*"

## INTEGRATING THE INFORMATION TRIANGLE

Infopreneurs who successfully integrate the Information Triangle within organizations must wear several hats:

- *Project sponsor*—to make sure the project gets adequate funding.
- *Project champion*—to make sure the project has someone who can sell the idea to others.
- *Project manager*—to make sure the administrative details are attended to.
- *Project implementor*—to integrate the design, technology, and manpower into a working model.

The most common error that occurs when integrating the Information Triangle is letting the technological priorities outdistance the organizational consequences. Rarely do computers, telephones, or credit cards cause work to cease. Instead, the problem centers on the fact that people do not know how to effectively utilize the technology. In this case, the infopreneur must subordinate the technology to the business strategy and the human resource management factors. As people become comfortable with the functions of the Information Triangle, the organization achieves a new business structure.

A well-defined methodology can help integrate the Information Triangle. Technological advances start with the need to provide a better solution to an existing problem. Quite often infopreneurs, engineers, and enterprising investors integrate the Information Triangle into a product or service for the marketplace along the lines of the following steps:

## Step 1:  The Idea

Technological breakthroughs such as the Information Triangle all start as creative ideas. Specific and detailed measurement criteria help determine the validity of a new idea:

- Can it be absorbed into the exisiting business structure?
- Does it leverage corporate assets?
- Does it align with market trends?

## Step 2:  The Research

Research varies in format, content, and sophistication. Research designs range from bootlegging to book-length reports. Three questions should be answered by your research:

- What is the size of the market?
- Is the timing right for meeting the need?
- Is the technology adequate?

## Step 3:  The Market Test

Testing provides insights into the feasibility of the Information Triangle. It helps select the best method to meet the specifications. Testing validates ideas and provides a window of opportunity to obtain patents, secure financing, and eliminate problems. During the testing period, technical specialists should design the best way to integrate the Information Triangle into the exisiting business structure. Technical specialists on the project should include:

- *Phone companies*—regarding telecommunications capabilities and available exchanges.
- *Computer vendors*—regarding information management technology and audiotext capabilities.
- *Local bankers*—regarding credit card processing and electronic funds transfer applications.

The test phase should produce a prototype of an effective Information Triangle and communicate with a cross section of the market to be serviced.

## Step 4:   The Business Plan

Once the testing phase reveals the most effective route, the business plan helps define the steps required to successfully implement the Information Triangle. A business plan should contain the following elements:

- A detailed description of primary and secondary markets.
- A list of benefits derived from implementing the Information Triangle.
- A description of resources that make up the Information Triangle.
- A summary of how the Information Triangle resolves specific problems.
- An overview of how the Information Triangle fits into the corporate strategy.
- A summary about how the Information Triangle will be introduced and marketed.
- An analysis of how the Information Triangle differentiates services and products in light of present and future competition.
- A set of technical and business benchmarks that corresponds to timelines and financial expenditures.
- A summary of how the project is organized and staffed.
- A list of risks, contingency plans, and abort points.
- An analysis of the Information Triangle's technological life cycle.

# TECHNOLOGIES OF THE INFORMATION TRIANGLE

When infopreneurs integrate the Information Triangle (telephone/computer/electronic funds transfer union), they must start with an understanding of its full range of technological capabilities:

## Telephones

Moving information in the form of data is growing five times as fast as voice and will represent 60 percent of all telephone line traffic by 1995 compared with only 15 percent in 1985.

- *800 Numbers*—Three significant applications of toll-free WATS lines include: providing answers through a total information center, establishing relationships through direct response marketing, and tracking the effectiveness of advertising campaigns through in-bound lines.
- *900 Numbers*—Polling and information lines can generate information to or from thousands of people at the same time.
- *976 Dial-it Numbers*—Short taped programs that bring mass access to specialized information and entertainment.
- *700 Numbers*—Interactive system handles conference calling with up to 58 participants at the same time.
- *Sponsored Services*—Charitable or medical information available through hotline phone numbers.
- *Subscription Services*—Information services that charge a monthly access fee.
- *Talking Yellow Pages*—Free directory assistance about local businesses to consumers.
- *Voice Messaging Services*—Service bureaus that act as information intermediaries.

## Computers

This technological phenomenon has become the fastest and most cost-efficient way to store, manage, and communicate information:

- *Storage*—The magnetic digital media used to store information include computer tapes, data cartridges, data modules, diskettes, disk packs, and optical digital disks.
- *Management*—Systems technology include computer-assisted indexing (provides automated indexing of active or archive information) and computer assisted locator

(uses bar code scanning and automated indexing to track information).

- *Communication*—In order to communicate information that has been generated, stored, and managed, three pieces of equipment are required: a modem (allows computers to talk with each other), a cable (connects modems to computers), and software (works according to menus or status screens).

## Electronic Funds Transfer

By 1995 up to half of all U.S. payments will be made electronically through banks, credit cards, phone companies, the Federal Reserve, and private clearinghouses.

- *Banks*—In 1985 more than a half-billion electronic transactions were executed among financial institutions.
- *Credit cards*—Increased competition among financial institutions, volatile interest rates, and new technology are responsible for the increased number of credit cards. More than 212 million credit cards are in use alone through Visa, MasterCard, American Express, and Sears.
- *Phone companies*—They co-produce Dial-it messages, report on activity, bill customers, collect monies, and forward payment on to the infopreneur or corporation.
- *Federal Reserve*—The Federal Reserve electronically processes payments between banks.
- *Private clearinghouses*—Compete with the Federal Reserve and are projected to execute up to 20 billion annual transactions by 1999.

Even the $80 billion per year nonprofit sector is turning to the Information Triangle to improve its fundraising effectiveness. The trend among donor-based nonprofit organizations is to stimulate new income activity from among the core donors.

Although most organizations have major gift fundraising projects and programs directed to their entire mailing lists, few have found ways to personally communicate with large numbers of donors on a consistent basis to give greater amounts. The Information Triangle has become a cost-effective compromise between personal visits and direct mail fundraising. A telephone call with a tape recorded message lets leaders of organizations communicate one-on-one with donors to explain the need as only they can do it. The Information Triangle helps these religious, political, and humanitarian organizations raise more funds than ever before.

Often no capital investment is required to integrate this dynamic into the fundraising activities. A computer manages all telephone activity and telephone scripts. When a supporter is called on the phone and responds with a donation or a monthly pledge, the money can be obtained over the phone by simply requesting the donor's credit card number and the amount they wish to give. When this occurs, the organization receives its revenue immediately. A computerized letter can be sent thanking the donor for the gift and reinforcing the importance of their support.

Integrating the Information Triangle into a television fundraising program can transform the broadcast's mass media into a personalized, interactive media. Those who call in pledges can even request to have their donations on a monthly basis electronically transferred from their account to the organization without the donor ever having to write a check.

In many cases, information technology is characterized by overestimating what can be accomplished in the short term, combined with underestimating its long term consequences. However, infopreneurs have integrated the Information Triangle to actually change the way business is conducted and impact consumer behavior.

The computer/telephone/electronic funds transfer union is a vital dynamic that creates a competitive advantage as it facilitates the movement of information and money. The Information Triangle alters the way information is delivered, eliminates expensive intermediaries, improves information's value, and changes the way infopreneurs turn data into dollars.

# HERE'S HOW BY
# WHO'S WHO

Infopreneurs, motivated by a spirit of adventure, create new technologies, new types of information, and new ways to do business. Rather than imitating their successes, integrate into your own experience the feelings and insights of other infopreneurs so you too can create, succeed, and turn data into dollars.

You have probably heard the story about the ambitious young infopreneur who called up a very successful infopreneur and asked about his secret to success. The elder infopreneur answered, "The secret to my success comes down to having good judgment."

Not satisfied with the curt answer the persistent young-ster responded, "How did you get all of that good judg-ment?" Thinking for a moment the infopreneur answered, "Experience."

Still not satisfied, the young man asked, "How did you get all of that experience?" Without hesitation the agitated info-preneur exclaimed, "Poor judgment!"

It is not just experience, poor judgment, a good idea, or hard work that makes an infopreneur. At the foundation of almost all infopreneurial success lie three key factors: risk, trust, and commitment.

Infopreneurs *risk* when they take a stand for what they believe is a good idea. Within this context of risk, it takes a fortuitous combination of elements and timing, hard work and good luck. It is not unusual for the infopreneur to risk and fail many times before their idea or product is accepted. Tenacity and persistence are prerequisites when taking a unique idea to market. Tough times are part of the process and to be expected when risking. Infopreneurs must learn early on how to weather the storms to make these tough times less traumatic.

The second factor of infopreneurial success is *trust*. Any-time people buy information, the transaction is based on a personal relationship—people trusting each other. The trust-ing relationship is as important as the accuracy of the informa-tion itself. Successful infopreneurs project the image that customers buying their information are buying the standard by which the industry is judged.

Finally, to succeed as an infopreneur requires *commitment*. Remember, it takes everything to be an infopreneur that it takes to be an entrepreneur, plus an ability to work with data and information technology. Infopreneurs are not just people with good ideas. They make their ideas happen. If you are not one of the "make it happen" people, accept the fact, then go out and find a partner who is. Be sure you are also committed to making a profit. This commitment requires the infopreneur to be constantly looking for new ways to simultaneously lower costs and maximize revenues.

# STARTING AN INFORMATION BUSINESS

An information business starts with an idea. Once the idea is crystallized, establish a clear-cut and quantifiable goal. Next, define a strategy and measurement criteria to monitor the progress toward the goal. Finally, follow these nine steps to structure your infopreneurial venture:

1. Take the market's pulse.
2. Define the business structure.
3. Obtain start-up financing.
4. Design the marketing program.
5. Acquire needed equipment.
6. Locate the best site.
7. Recruit a qualified staff.
8. Obtain needed supplies.
9. Assess insurance needs.

Infopreneurs handle differently the challenges of starting and operating an information business. Since there are no concrete rules for turning data into dollars, we shall explore the myriad of options to starting an information business.

## Take the Market's Pulse

Before taking off with an idea, obtain feedback from the marketplace, especially from people you trust. Start by approaching your customers, vendors, suppliers, and technicians. These are people who can provide firsthand feedback as to the feasibility of the new idea. Next, interview librarians and consultants to obtain an overview of the marketplace niches and understand the full potential of the idea. Then, check with lawyers, accountants, bankers, and federal/state agencies to structure and finance the idea.

It is not unusual for infopreneurs to conceptualize unique businesses. Driven by the need to translate the idea into

**Steps to Start Your Information Business**

**1. Take the Market Pulse**
- Customers
- Vendors
- Suppliers
- Technicians
- Librarians
- Consultants
- Lawyers
- Bankers
- Fed/State Agencies

**2. Define Business Structure**
- Sole Proprietor
- Partnership
- Subchapter S
- Corporation

**3. Obtain Start-up Financing**
- Personal Funds
- Investors
- Public Stock Sale
- Venture Capital
- Bank Loans

**4. Design Marketing Program**
- Research
- Positioning
- Promotion
- Pricing
- Sales

**5. Acquire Needed Equipment**
- Needs
- Software
- Hardware
- Staff
- Vendors
- Lease/Buy
- Install
- Service

**6. Locate Best Site**
- Comfortable
- Inter-changeable
- Accessible
- Visible

**7. Recruit Qualified Staff**
- Description
- Recruitment
- Training
- Performance
- Compensation

**8. Obtain Needed Supplies**
- Quality
- Quantity
- Price
- Terms
- Vendors

**9. Assess Insurance Needs**
- Needs
- Options
- Purchase

Copyright: Foresight and Planning, 1987.

156

reality, they often commit their attention, energy, and re-sources to bring forth the new concept without receiving market input. Not seeking market input or listening to the advice of self-appointed "experts" brands infopreneurs as "bull headed" in their approach to launching their business.

Once the infopreneur conceptualizes an information prod-uct or service, he needs to plug into the network of people who can help. For example, one infopreneur took a Small Business Administration volunteer to lunch every week to discuss his idea. The volunteer asked questions for which the infopreneur did not have answers. Success in business became correlated to the infopreneur's ability to find answers to those questions.

Another infopreneur read *The Third Wave* by futurist Alvin Toffler. He tried to conceptualize his business from Toffler's point of view. Then he called Toffler to set up a meeting. They met three times over seven days to discuss the infopreneurial venture.

Often when an infopreneur takes the pulse of the market, the news is not welcomed! One infopreneur heard repeatedly that his idea would not work and that he should not even attempt it. He considered the advice, then committed to try-ing the idea. He is now in his fifth year of business.

Market input can be as simple as a single bit of focused advice such as, "Nothing happens with information until sales occur," or as complex as having a technologist design from scratch a new computer system.

Creative and persistent networking is critical in the success of infopreneurial ventures. Others must know what is being developed or marketed. And the well-established network pro-vides momentum, credibility, and exposure for the new idea.

Failure to receive adequate input will result in a company becoming insular. One infopreneur lamented the fact that he should have depended more on people who understood his industry first then learned the technology, rather than on tech-nologists who could later learn his industry.

One way to compensate experts who become involved in your venture when your cash flow is low, is to give them a stake in the future in exchange for their help early on.

A subtle downside risk lurks in seeking market input. The

infopreneur can become "outer directed." In essence, the emotional drive that comes from bringing a new idea to market can be substituted with the adulation of others for the idea. Unfortunately, the infopreneur often settles for the emotional reinforcement from the feedback rather than viewing it as a means to fulfilling the new idea.

## Define Business Structure

The basic information business structures, or forms of ownership, include proprietorships, partnerships, and corporations.

More than three-fourths of all American enterprises are proprietorships—businesses owned and managed by an individual. Many people establish this form of ownership because it is simple to create, inexpensive to establish, profits go to the owner, involve minimal legal restrictions, and the owner makes all decisions.

However, there are several disadvantages inherent in this form of ownership: unlimited personal liability, limited organizational or corporate skills, limited access to capital, and lack of business continuity (the business ceases when the owner retires or dies).

Infopreneurs often begin as sole proprietorships because they are small and wish to avoid the encumbrances of the corporation. But once the information product takes off, revenues increase, and new possibilities of risk are introduced. So infopreneurs often transition into a corporate structure to more effectively function.

A partnership is an association of two or more persons who engage in business as co-owners sharing the assets and liabilities of the business, and the profits, according to the terms of the partnership agreement. Advantages of partnerships are that they are easy to create with minimal government regulations, the profits are divided according to the agreement, they have access to larger pools of capital, they have the ability to draw new talent or limited partners, and business income is taxed as individual income.

Disadvantages of the partnership form of ownership include: unlimited liability of the general partners, capital accumulation is limited, difficulty in disposing of partnership interest without dissolving the partnership, the partnerships lack continuity, and authority conflicts are not uncommon.

It is important to find a partner who is different than you are—inside/outside, night/day, promoter/accountant, conservative/risk taker. The key is to share the same vision. One infopreneurial venture which became an international success consisted of four partners with different functions: an inside man, an outside man, a business man, and a computer genius.

A corporation, the most complex of the three major forms of business ownership, stands as a separate legal entity. Generally, a corporation must report its financial operations to the state's attorney general on an annual basis. If stock of the corporation is sold in more than one state, the corporation must comply with federal regulations governing the sale of securities.

Advantages of the corporation include limited stockholder liability, an ability to attract large amounts of capital, ease of ownership transfer, and access to large pools of skill, talent, and information.

Disadvantages of corporations include: the time and expense to incorporate, corporate taxes, legal restrictions, and loss of control by the corporate founders.

Corporations are popular forms of ownership for infopreneurs. Many information businesses appreciate the image-enhancement and credibility they acquire with a corporation. Others appreciate the tax benefits the corporate shell provides. While many use the corporation to take their information product public and obtain investor dollars early on, others use this legal entity to limit their liability and spread their risk.

The popular "hybrid" form of corporate ownership seen among infopreneurs is the Subchapter S corporation which is insulated from federal income taxes. Consequently, the earnings are taxed only as individual income to the infopreneur.

As a Subchapter S corporation the infopreneur can set up the venture with a minimum of paperwork and expense. Another benefit is that the infopreneur can remain as principal sharesholder in order to take the losses and profits personally. One infopreneur, who holds an M.B.A. in accounting from

Stanford, designed his venture as a Subchapter S to personally account for the initial losses. He also felt that he could better shelter his funds at the personal level than at the corporate level.

## Obtain Start-Up Financing

Capital, which is any form of wealth used to produce more wealth, exists in a typical business as cash, inventory, equipment, or plant. The three basic types of capital include fixed, working, and growth capital.

Fixed capital is used to purchase permanent assets of a business such as buildings, land, computers, and other equipment. Working capital is the capital used to keep the business operating on a short term basis. Growth capital is required when a business expands or changes its primary direction. These three types of capital must be kept separate during the financial planning of an information business.

A business start-up which grows quickly, has available to it three types of money known as equity, long-term debt, and lines of credit.

The sources of equity, with financing vehicles in parentheses, include the nonprofessional investor (partnership formation, stock issue), venture capitalist (stock issue), and SBIC-MESBIC (convertible debenture, debt with warrants).

The sources for long-term debt include banks (term loan-limited, unsecured term loan, equipment loan, equipment leasing, real estate loan), SBIC-MESBIC (term loan-limited, unsecured term loan, equipment loan, equipment leasing), commercial finance company (equipment loan, equipment leasing, real estate loan), life insurance company (policy loan, real estate loan), savings and loan association (real estate loan), leasing (equipment leasing), consumer finance company (personal property term loan), Small Business Administration (term loan guarantee), Economic Development Administration (direct term loan-limited), and local development company (facilities/equipment financing).

Sources for lines of credit include suppliers (trade credit), bank (unsecured line of credit, accounts receivable financing, inventory financing, flooring, indirect collection financing), commercial finance company (accounts receivable financing, inventory financing, factoring), factor (factoring), Small Business Administration (line of credit guarantee-limited).

### Personal Funds

The most popular form of start-up financing for infopreneurs is personal funds. When launching a venture with personal funds, the business is commonly referred to as a "bootstrap venture."

Bootstrapping is a fantastic way to start an information business because when it succeeds, the infopreneur can consider it the ultimate business achievement. One infopreneur started with $5000 and spent it all on direct mail. He figured if not enough people signed up for his information service, he would return their money and go on to something else. The direct mail test succeeded and the venture has been self-funding ever since.

Consider the benefits of starting with little or no outside money. It forces the infopreneur to think strategically. Self-funding actually tests the commitment level. Unless infopreneurs believe in their ideas and are willing to totally commit to them in the early rounds, they should invest their futures elsewhere.

Self-funding infopreneurs range from those having affluent clients whose billings cover the start-up costs, to the infopreneur, who with 13 consecutive business failures, as the story goes, borrowed $20,000 from 12 credit cards and rolled it out on his idea . . . this time he won.

One benefit of bootstrapping is that you cannot afford to make big mistakes early on. A direct correlation seems to exist between the amount of money you have invested at the start of the venture and the amount of learning you will do.

### Investors

Infopreneurs need to realize that there is never a money problem only an "idea" problem. There are often plenty of friends and family members who will invest in a good idea. When a venture requires $750,000 to get started you tend to tap anyone with interest in the idea.

One of the risks involved with a new information venture is the chance that it might not work. One infopreneur who lost $400,000 of his personal funds and an equal amount of his family's money comments, "Do you know what Thanksgivings are like each year?"

One suggestion is that rather than borrowing money from a computer programmer or accountant, for example, ask them to contribute their talents in exchange for equity in the venture.

### Bank Loans, Venture Capital, Public Stock Sales

One of the secrets to working with banks is showing them up front how they will be paid back. Once this is adequately explained, they will examine your track record of successes. If they are convinced you can do what you say, they will carefully inspect your business plan. A record of established customers can be helpful in building credibility. However, several infopreneurs have received bank loans based on customer commitments for contracts.

When preparing a proforma for an information business, a good rule of thumb is to double everything on the negative side and halve everything on the positive side. In other words, double your expenses and halve your income expectations.

Raising money, getting credit, or selling stock requires a good business plan. So after completing your forecasts, determine your figure for time and expenses, and then double it!

Once a budget is established, police yourself stoically to stick to it. You will probably realize that your start-up money is inadequate. Information businesses often take a year or more to get off the ground. Do not plan to run the business and live the good life out of the operational profits in the beginning.

One infopreneur suggested stocking plenty of peanut butter when you start. Being hungry in the beginning is positive because it makes you hustle. But if you are starving after a year, step back and reconsider your strategy. Perhaps you should bring on a business partner with credibility in the world of finance. If your idea is still solid, the partner will help in approaching new investors.

Unexpected events can be quite challenging to infopreneurs in the beginning of a new venture. For example, one info-preneur invested one million dollars in an on-line system that would provide more information directly to his clients. After its first year, the infopreneur accounted for the project and realized that his new information service generated only 5 percent of his income, while drawing upon 25 percent of his corporate resources. The moral? Be smart; be flexible; and, hang on.

## Design Marketing Program

Infopreneurial marketing is the process of delivering informa-tion to customers. The primary function of marketing is to identify markets the infopreneur plans to service and uncover niches to exploit. The marketing concept contains research, positioning, promotion, pricing, and sales.

### Research

Market research is a tool to help infopreneurs identify poten-tial customers, determine needs and wants, and ascertain what these customers are willing to pay for information. An infopreneur's market research does not have to be sophisti-cated to be valuable. The goal of research is to understand a venture's upside potential and downside risks. Applied re-search ultimately improves decision making and provides a competitive edge.

Research starts by determining the specific nature of the problem that needs to be investigated. Data should be col-lected from any and all available resources and analyzed, then conclusions drawn.

Start your research by going to businesses or consumers to ask if your information would be helpful to them. If so, ask the price it would be worth. Taking a market survey can actually help companies see where they stand in their information gathering expertise. After completing a market survey, one infopreneur pointed out the company's need for more competitive coverage in its information gathering process. So he was paid to give it to them.

Through market research, one infopreneur found that he could expand the market for his information by using the same analysis methodology, but simply changing a few of the variables.

Basic market research should let you know the types of markets for your information: "pull-through" businesses, where a market already exists for the data, or "push through" businesses where you try to create a market. If you determine that the market is "push through" consider your options: Keep looking until you find a "pull through" market, reposition the information so it becomes acceptable to the market, or go broke trying to create a market that may not exist.

Your best research will come from clients you are currently servicing. Stay close to them to identify and satisfy their emerging needs.

### Positioning

Positioning is an organized system for finding windows in the mind of your market. In an overcommunicated society, positioning helps improve communications. Infopreneurs become "positioned" when they understand the mind of their constituents, their own strengths and weaknesses, and the strengths and weaknesses of their competitors.

The easiest way to get into the mind of the market is to be first with your information. The first infopreneur to occupy a position in the mind is difficult to dislodge. Once there, an infopreneur must concentrate on never giving customers a reason to switch.

An important rule of positioning can be paraphrased that it is better to be a big fish in a small pond (and then increase the size of the pond) than to be a small fish in a big pond.

Positioning starts with the early recognition of a problem and placing your information as its perfect solution. One infopreneur realized that since there were not any competitors in the value-added industry he helped pioneer, he became the industry standard. When his customers were asked their immediate reactions when they think of him, they commented, "He provides fast, cheap, and understandable information." This stature is the position he owns in the mind of his market.

### Promotion

The bottom line to profitable promotions is that the sales expense becomes a smaller percentage of sales as the promotion expense becomes a larger percentage of the sales expense. Promotions can bring in new customers, upgrade occasional users to regular customers, reposition the competition, upgrade the dollar volume per purchase, and cross-sell other information products and service.

Promotion starts by becoming visible to the right people. This should include such activities as writing articles for professional journals, becoming a member and presenter to key organizations, and placing your venture in a newsworthy context so it receives free coverage from newspapers and magazines.

One advantage of well-executed promotions is that they tend to attract the serious buyer, whereas advertising tends to deliver a larger percentage of lookers.

If your efforts to generate newsworthy publicity fail, consider hiring a good, hard-hitting public relations firm to help position and promote you.

After the publicity slows, extend your exposure by placing ads. If an ad seems unproductive, try another angle or a different medium. When something works, stick with it. One infopreneur tested many options until he found that his ads pulled best in college newspapers. Another infopreneur placed ads on a nationwide basis in law journals which instantly generated business and stimulated his cash flow.

However, many infopreneurs will discover that broad-based advertising is not a good investment. Becoming visible to the right people is the key. This targeting may start by picking out who you want to contact, then take the initiative. One infopreneur finds his "hardest working dollars" go into direct mail and phone calls, while another uses the phone and computer because they are "quick and clean."

One infopreneur even offers prospects one free month of service to try his interactive information service. This trial period puts his prospects on-line and gives them experience with the system. He created the promotion because there was no previous demand for such a service.

### Pricing

Pricing is the mechanism for allocating information among potential customers and to ensure competition among sellers in an open market economy. In the information business, price can vary from a monopoly market at its introduction to market auction prices at the point of saturation.

Price can be adjusted for the level of customer and producer involvement. The complexity to create and distribute information can also impact information's price. To successfully price your information, you must understand your customers, competitors, and internal capabilities.

Most infopreneurs price their information according to what the market will bear. In one situation, an infopreneur saw his information change from monopoly prices to market auction prices in less than a decade because of breakthroughs in technology.

Some infopreneurs price low to get a full workload, then up their prices to weed out less profitable customers. Other infopreneurs price information low to get customers in, then keep them in through performance. Still others price low to focus on the broad-based mass markets, and avoid the customized and high-priced niche.

The high-priced infopreneurs also have a variety of motives. Some price high so as not to give themselves away. Others find the high price allows them to fall back or cut deals when the demand is elastic.

In a competitive market, where the same information is available from more than one source, infopreneurs must price information according to what the alternative information sources charge, keeping in mind what the market will bear. To be successful with a competitive-based pricing strategy, the infopreneur must focus on providing *better* and *better* information to *more* and *more* people at *lower* and *lower* costs.

The pricing mechanism as a function of internal capabilities takes various forms. One infopreneur prices his information according to what a marketing staff employee would be paid to spend one month on the job for generating a comparable report. Another infopreneur prices according to the total expenses of outside vendors plus his overhead. Still another charges on a per search basis of his data base, whether he carries the information or not.

### Sales

In the information business, nothing happens until a sale occurs. In other words, any information business, large or small, cannot survive unless people are willing to pay for information. Develop a sales strategy to gain a competitive edge with your information. For example, with a market penetration strategy, an infopreneur seeks to improve sales of existing information in current markets through better sales and promotional efforts. A market development strategy requires an infopreneur to increase sales by introducing current information into new markets. With a product development strategy an infopreneur tries to increase sales volume by creating new information products and services for existing markets.

When starting out in business, a good sales strategy is to quickly establish a couple of key reference accounts. Getting customers early on enhances credibility because it proves you can translate your information into a checkwriting process.

It is unusual to find the ideal information product. But occasionally it does happen. Some infopreneurs have found that their information fills so many niches and needs, that they do not even need publicity or advertising to generate sales. If this is the case, word-of-mouth advertising stimulates the market activity.

Once sales start to accumulate, remember to focus on the characteristics of your most profitable clients. You will find these "quality" clients buying your information repeatedly. Be sure to obtain referrals from these sources.

To be successful in selling information, infopreneurs generally attempt 30 or 40 different ways to sell their information products and services. You have to continually think about the markets the information will be sold in, the cost of reaching these people, and the potential return on investment. If there is truly a need for the information, a profitable way of selling it may be just around the corner.

Remember, sales are the fulcrum of infoprenurial success. Culminating the first sale will help everything else fall into place. If customers are not pursuing your information, approach them with it.

## Acquire Needed Equipment

Equipment purchases that range from desktop telephones to multimillion dollar computers require detailed planning so that infopreneurs buy not only what is needed today, but systems that will expand with their businesses into the future.

When purchasing a new computer, for example, start by performing a needs analysis. Write a detailed description of what the information system will do. Include the types of reports required and the features preferred.

Once the *needs* for a computer are listed, consider the software that will likely match these needs. Look at industry standard software as well as software for which there are not yet standard packages. Operating software usually comes with the hardware purchase while specialty software, which molds a system to a particular operation and management style, are purchased separately.

When buying hardware, consider the computer system itself, the peripherals, office furniture, cards, tapes, and manuals that accompany the system. Develop a checklist to compare the contents of vendor bids. Plan a time for the staff to test the equipment. Ask vendors for a list of customers who own the same or similar hardware configurations. Have ready a list of questions to ask these computer owners.

The staff should be involved in the evaluation of the equipment and the decision to purchase a system. Make sure they have plenty of hands-on practice and are comfortable with the technology. Involve the staff in training, buying of supplies and furniture, establishing a work plan for use of the computer, and a review of their progress on the computer. The decision to purchase a computer is only the beginning of the process. Realize that people are ultimately the most expensive investment in automation. So choose a computer with your staff in mind.

When dealing with vendors, understand their policies and practices; get written commitments; learn about volume discounts and minimum charges; ask for protection against price increases; understand their credit and return policies for faulty hardware or software; be sure to check references; have the proposed contract reviewed by a lawyer, accountant, and someone who has purchased a similar system; get a copy of a vendor invoice to see just how and what they bill for.

How to acquire a computer system is predominantly a financial decision rather than a technical or operational one. A purchased computer has depreciation value as a capital asset. The computer hardware and software that is part of a turnkey system can be claimed as an investment tax credit. There are special first-year expenses of tangible personal property. The interest expenses associated with the financing of the system can also be deducted.

Should the computer be leased, all lease payments are fully deductible and the investment tax credits can be negotiated with the lessor. Leasing helps preserve cash flow, capital, and bank credit lines.

When installing a computer allow adequate floor space. Raised floors are often required for larger computers that depend on special air conditioning and power lines. Be sure to provide sufficient electrical power for the system, as well as property and systems insurance coverage.

When considering a computer warranty and service contract, consider the value of the service firm. Ask them to help isolate and reduce the sources of waste found within most information systems by getting the best rates available, tapping into the current resources, fully utilizing the current system, and maximizing personnel efficiency.

Some infopreneurs prefer to build their own computer equipment rather than buy it from vendors or retailers. These technocrats and do-it-yourselfers have different motivations. Some feel that they are state-of-the art. Others describe their homemade equipment, not as being on the "cutting edge," but on the "bleeding edge" of progress. Still other infopreneurs design their equipment so that they are applications-oriented. In one case, the infopreneur writes his own software to better meet his application requirements.

In any case, infopreneurs design their own equipment not for the sake of designing equipment, but for the uses that the new technology offers.

When one infopreneur could not find the interface equipment he needed, he just built the interface himself. Another infopreneur looked for ways to reduce his costs and still accomplish his business application. He built his own computer, became a low-cost provider of information and increased his corporate profits.

Another infopreneur inferred the technology life cycle of a computer to be around 18 months. He makes productivity gains by jumping into the newest systems.

The philosophies of owning equipment vary from infopreneur to infopreneur. Regardless of the type, most infopreneurs consider equipment not just the tools of the trade, but as symbols of their commitment to their business mission. And even though the capital costs may be sizable, rarely do they cut corners.

Most infopreneurs strive to make their information universally applicable. Therefore they generally operate within the MS-DOS environment with either IBM or other top name technology.

After infopreneurs consider the technology's applications, they carefully analyze the economics of the buying decision. In one case, the infopreneur concluded that if the technology drops the cost of a particular operation by 50 percent or more, it is worth purchasing.

Support is important. When buying a computer, infopreneurs should get the best professional help available. Many times this requires buying computer equipment retail so as to take advantage of the local support and service.

Infopreneurs succeed in the information business when the information they generate translates into dollars in the pockets of their customers. To become proficient problem-solvers in the market infopreneurs need to take time to understand their equipment and learn the word processing, spreadsheet, data base management, and desktop publishing software. Most infopreneurs subscribe to five or six computer magazines to stay conversant and up to date. In the words of one infopreneur, "There is a direct financial gain for this extra effort."

There are three ways to look at spending money on equipment: First, it is easier to spend money than it is to make money. In starting up a business, infopreneurs need to minimize the front end cash outflow any way possible. Before you buy, lease, and before you lease, try to rent your equipment. With this strategy, not only can you keep costs down, but you can also acquire the needed experience and training at the least cost.

Second, when starting out, you need less purchased equipment than you think. Before buying equipment, ask yourself how much money you are willing to lose if the business does not get off the ground. Then look at where this money can best be spent.

Third, even though the computer may provide many answers, save time, and cost a lot of money, watch out for your phone system—it could eventually become your biggest equipment expense.

## Locate Best Site

The four principles of running a retail business include accessibility, surplus parking, visibility, and inventory. A business must be accessible to its customers. It must provide its clients surplus parking. (If parking is only adequate, chances are it will be insufficient.) The company must be visible so people are aware it is in business. Finally, customers must be provided with the proper inventory to meet their needs.

However, the four principles of operating an information business are quite different from running a retail business. Infopreneurs have created the principles of infopreneurship to most effectively turn data into dollars. For infopreneurs, the location is still a high priority, but for reasons other than the needs of the customer. An infopreneur must be comfortable in the location, be it at home in the country or in a glass building from the heart of the business district. The location must be comfortable.

The reasons for setting up an information business in certain locations range from productivity gains to recreation, from taxes to time savings. One infopreneur located his office in his home because it increased his output at a lower cost, while another infopreneur, who wanted to play 90 softball games a year, moved his business from Chicago to Atlanta.

One infopreneur located away from the city to avoid the taxes, while another put his office just ten minutes from his house to be closer to his family. Since many infopreneurs find working from home most comfortable, they are faced with the challenges of workaholism and distractions. Self-discipline is the key to working from home. Successful home-based infopreneurs set out to accomplish a predetermined result each day.

Next, the location must be interchangeable. In other words, the infopreneur must be able to carry the office from one location to another. Often this requires only an electrical outlet to supply power to a computer and a telephone to contact clients. Infopreneurs who work from an office often have a room at home where the same work can be accomplished.

In most cases the infopreneur's home becomes interchangeable with the office. One infopreneur used an extra bedroom in his mother-in-law's house to set up his information venture. The bedroom contained a computer, telephones, and beeper machines. Another infopreneur downloads data at night in his living room at one-tenth the cost of daytime business hours. Home becomes an effective interchangeable site because everything tends to be in one place. Many infopreneurs differentiate their offices from their homes by activity. They do their work at the office and all of their study and reading at home.

Shared business spaces are becoming a popular alternative for interchangeability. These spaces provide infopreneurs with phones, computers, copy machines, even secretarial services, and many require only a three-month commitment.

Since infopreneurs are not dependent on walk-in traffic, they do not need to provide easy access to their location. However, proximity to an airport is a high priority because clients of successful infopreneurs are often located in other states and countries. Even though most correspondence is by phone and computer, occasionally the infopreneur must venture out for a face-to-face encounter with clients.

Infopreneurs seem to locate either right in the center of their market or far away from the action. Most infopreneurs consider the information business a people business in which they require quick access to their contacts and customers. It is not a bad business practice to locate yourself as close as possible to the market you are selling to. However, with telecommunications you can choose to locate almost anywhere and always stay in touch.

As for infopreneurs not located close to their market, they still have the need to be close to an airport because of that rare instance when they must visit with clients in person.

Visibility can include everything from a recognizable address to having the name of the infopreneur mentioned in the *Wall Street Journal*. The old adage, "exposure creates opportunity," holds true today for infopreneurs.

For one infopreneur, his office site in Manhattan was relatively unimportant. What was important, though, was getting his venture to work in New York because of the visibility and credibility that success in that city would lend to his venture. Another infopreneur required the prestige of the 212 and 800 telephone prefixes for his venture. He simply located his data entry on Long Island to keep his costs down.

## Recruit Qualified Staff

Most infopreneurs openly confess that the growth and success of their businesses are dependent upon competent employees. Staffing an infopreneurial venture is a critical part of business that requires job descriptions, recruitment and selection of staff, training and monitoring of performance, and of course, compensation.

### Job Description

A job description details the job, its duties, responsibilities, and the work conditions. Where a job is performed and how

173

the duties should be executed are often part of the job description. Job specifications, on the other hand, describe the type of person best suited to fill the position, including the applicant's education, skill and experience levels, as well as personal characteristics.

Infopreneurs design job descriptions to set forth the duties and job specifications that translate these duties into qualifications necessary to perform the duties.

Infopreneurs often describe a job as having impact, as something exciting, as a unique opportunity to do something that others have not done, or as a career in which they can take pride. One infopreneur goes so far as to say that he hates employees, rather he wants participants in his ideas.

The job description should start by selling the candidate on the challenge of the work—money, prestige, and titles all follow.

On a practical level, one infopreneur has no employees because of all the paper work. Instead he is staffed completely with private contractors.

### Recruitment and Selection

When the need for a qualified employee arises, the most logical place to begin the search is among current employees at the business. Promoting from within motivates employees and retains qualified people.

A second source of qualified information handlers is from among the competition. Hiring an employee away from a competitor not only fills the needed slot, but also offers the chance to obtain valuable knowledge into the operations of a competitor.

A third place to find qualified employees is through schools. The entry-level employee force is a good source of potential candidates, especially from community colleges and technical education centers.

A fourth source of employees is from the business marketplace. These include newspapers and trade magazines, private and state employment agencies, walk-in candidates, former employees, as well as recommendations of current staff members.

Infopreneurs have some specific ideas about recruiting and

selecting employees. For example, one infopreneur recruits and contracts with housewives for part-time work. Not only are these very conscientious employees but contracting keeps them off the payroll.

Another infopreneur considers senior citizens perfect employees for the information business. They are responsible, give a full return for the dollar, and rarely suffer the "head problems" associated with other age groups.

High school interns are recruited by another infopreneur. He finds them competent and motivated individuals who come in at entry-level pay scale.

Hiring of friends and family evokes mixed reactions. Some infopreneurs discourage hiring friends because of the risk of losing them in the end, yet others hire friends because they can be trusted. Whether it is family, friends, or strangers that you hire, the key is to insure that employees understand the goals for your infopreneurial venture.

Infopreneurs do not generally have problems hiring qualified employees for a couple of reasons. First, infopreneurs are on the cutting edge of the Information Revolution, so the times offer exciting opportunities for technicians. Second, information entrepreneurship is a contemporary business and a relatively sophisticated field which appeals to the industrious person.

### Training and Performance

Training is the key to growth and productivity in an information business. Learning new skills and acquiring new information are the only protections an information worker has against obsolescence.

Effective training stimulates productivity, improves morale of the work force, plants confidence within employees, and reduces waste which lowers the cost of doing business. Training is divided into two categories: on-the-job training and off-the-job training.

Most training within information businesses is classified as on-the-job. The most effective form of on-the-job training is when the owner or supervisor gets personally involved in the training of the staff.

Off-the-job training is accomplished through seminars, schooling, or work away from the job. Equipment vendors, Small Business Development Centers, community colleges, and technical or trade schools provide training in specialized areas important in a growing information business.

Evaluating the performance of an employee in an information business is a vital function of management. Performance appraisals should not be viewed as an annual ritual, but as an ongoing process. Appraisals are the control function for the firm's human resources and provide for both management and staff an opportunity for encouragement and correction.

The evaluation of appraisal is used to determine wage or salary increases, promotion, needed training, and overall job progress.

Infopreneurs often display several blind spots when it comes to training their employees. For example, many employees are attracted to the technology rather than the application. A business gains leverage when it can perform a function in repetition. Infopreneurs often become bored with the perfunctory activity of making money and move on to create new applications for new technologies.

A second blind spot develops when employees lose touch with the market. Get employees out of the office and into the market to meet with the users of the information. Employees must be trained to know what their customers need.

A third blind spot has to do with the employees' perception of their own roles in the venture. Some employees need to feel they are part of a team. Others need to be left alone as long as they are producing. Still others strive to become experts within the office. Finally, some employees like to have fun in their companies, which helps them produce and learn new skills.

### Compensation

Compensation is a complex formula that can provide both numeric as well as interpersonal comparisons. Compensation is one way employees gauge their progress in society. The tangible factors of compensation include wages and fringe benefits. Wages are determined by supply of and demand for the type of person seeking employment, federal and state minimum wage legislation, the cost of living in the geographic region, and the wage rate set by organized labor.

Fringe benefits for information workers often include life, medical, and disability insurance, company car, and a pension fund. Several observations should be made about compensation. First, information employees, depending on their skill level, are often paid well early on. Even though money is not the primary reason they work, tangible rewards help keep infopreneurs motivated.

Second, realize that there has to be a benefit for these workers beyond the paycheck. Employees need to be committed to the success of the business. Infopreneurs often structure compensation packages to account for accuracy and productivity, not just according to how much time they put in.

Third, beyond quarterly reviews for raises and bonuses, many infopreneurs make employees stockholders to give them a sense of ownership in the business.

## Obtain Needed Supplies

Keeping up on an inventory of supplies can be a problem area for many infopreneurs. Critical success factors in obtaining supplies include quality and quantity, price and terms, and vendors.

### Quality and Quantity

To purchase supplies of the right quality, the infopreneur must purchase items of a quality high enough to meet customer or production requirements, but not so high that they exceed specifications and create excessive costs. A quality product can be defined as one which conforms to predetermined standards.

Purchasing an excessive quantity of supplies is not a profitable investment because these dollars just sit on the shelf. Inventory should be viewed as a noninterest-bearing account. Maintaining a proper inventory is the result of careful planning, accurate monitoring, and tight managing of a company's supplies.

If you do not know how much inventory to carry, stay thin. In other words, buy everything day-to-day. One final thought about quality: when it comes to letterhead, go first class.

### Price and Terms

An infopreneur once told a customer, "You can have price or terms, but you can not have both. It is either your price and my terms or my price and your terms." The same holds true for obtaining supplies. Consider the value of cash discounts and catalog purchases versus buying on account at retail prices.

Use local wholesale stores to keep costs down. Be sure to shop around until you find the best price and service.

### Vendors

Once vendors and suppliers have been identified, the info-preneur must decide which ones to do business with. Some of the factors to consider when choosing a supplier include reliability, proximity, and service.

The infopreneur must evaluate the vendor's ability to deliver merchandise when it is needed. Late deliveries and shortages can create ill will and lost sales.

The vendor's physical proximity to the business is an important factor because distance often relates to the cost of the merchandise. Transportation costs are often passed on to the infopreneur in the form of higher prices.

The infopreneur must evaluate the range of services offered by vendors. Before choosing a supplier, question potential vendors about their knowledge of product lines, how they can assist in planning, their on-time delivery record, and any hints they can provide about purchasing supplies.

Finally, purchasing from more than one supplier is an important consideration. When buying from a single supplier, the infopreneur often receives special attention, quantity discounts, and cooperation from the supplier. However, purchasing from a number of vendors reduces the risk of losing control if something happens to the primary vendor. In addition, shopping for the best prices keeps vendors competitive.

Many infopreneurs select a good supplier and deal with

them on almost everything for simplicity. If you exercise this option, make sure the vendor gives you personal attention and delivers. Most infopreneurs depend on a competent wholesale office supply vendor who delivers the next day.

Most infopreneurs delegate the management of supplies to their employees so they can stay focused on the big picture. However, a good strategy is to buy everything first yourself, create a routine, then delegate it. One creative infopreneur made supplies a function of an employee's marketing success. Everytime he sold something he was rewarded with supplies from his wish list.

## Assess Insurance Needs

Insurance does not necessarily shield the infopreneur from risk. Infopreneurs must understand and evaluate the four risk strategies and choose one to function under.

The first is *risk avoidance* which involves staying clear of risky situations. This strategy is limited in its application since only a limited number of business risks can be avoided.

The second risk strategy is *risk reduction* which occurs when an infopreneur builds some degree of safety into risky situations. Examples are fire and theft precaution equipment.

The third risk strategy is *risk anticipation* which is a form of self-insurance; an infopreneur assumes the responsibility of risk. After reducing the risk level, the infopreneur sets aside funds to protect against such losses.

*Risk transfer* is the fourth strategy in which an infopreneur shifts the risk to another party, usually an insurance company. The infopreneur pays for insurance coverage and the company promises to pay a specific sum if a covered loss occurs.

The types of business insurance infopreneurs often purchase for their ventures include liability insurance which protects the infopreneur from losses resulting from accidents or losses while others are using their information; property insurance which protects the infopreneur against the loss, theft, or destruction of property through fire or flood, for example; surety insurance which provides protection for losses incurred by customers when an infopreneur fails to complete a contract correctly or on schedule; and crime insurance which protects the infopreneur from losses resulting from burglary, robbery, and employee theft.

To find the proper levels and types of insurance coverage, an infopreneur should choose an insurance agent who understands the firm's insurance needs and will cooperate to reduce the risks associated with turning data into dollars.

The three critical insurance concerns include equipment and data coverage, liability protection, and maintaining the integrity of the data.

The first consideration, protection of the equipment and data, is dealt with by carrying not only computer coverage, but also valuable papers coverage. Infopreneurs also protect their data by backing up their information off-site.

The second insurance consideration is that of liability. Anyone can sue an infopreneur for any reason. Getting it to hold up is something else. In other words, being sued and being liable are two different things. Many infopreneurs carry general liability coverage for their information and organizations. Most infopreneurs state their levels of liability in their contracts. This generally takes the form of a disclaimer on the information. Even though insurance is critical, consider the philosophy of one infopreneur, "If you buy half of what you are quoted, you'll probably have bought twice the amount you'll actually need."

One infopreneur buys coverage for "errors and omission." He says that it is not cheap but he does not like "running naked in front of attorneys."

The third consideration is insuring the quality of information. One infopreneur who downloads information from government data bases states in his contract that the quality of his information is only as good as its originating sources. Another infopreneur insures the quality of her information by verifying it over the phone. And still another infopreneur insures the quality of his information by always quoting primary sources. Finally, one infopreneur considers the best insurance for her information is a money-back guarantee. She gladly provides refunds if the customer is not totally satisfied.

This provides her an opportunity to learn about her business from disgruntled customers.

## CONCLUDING THOUGHTS

As we conclude Part One: Turning Data into Dollars, reflect on these thoughts. They could save you time and money or help you seize upon a new infopreneurial opportunity.

- *Commitment.* Unless you are willing to put yourself on the line 100 percent as an infopreneur, go back to being a contributing part of a corporation.
- *Customers.* Never take your customers for granted because they are always looking for new ways to do more for less.
- *Desire.* Find something that you can totally commit to because it will take all the tenacity and persistence you can muster to obtain it.
- *Focus.* Present sharply defined information to an extremely focused audience.
- *Ideas.* The simpler, the better. Be sure the infopreneurial idea is a natural extension of your personal interest.
- *Infopreneur.* It takes everything to be an infopreneur that it takes to be an entrepreneur, plus an ability to work with data and technology.
- *Information.* There is no shortage of information. Work to convert information into action-oriented knowledge.
- *Management.* Understand the difference between the innovation of an information product and the management of an information business.
- *Market response.* Beware of the "Wow!" People eat steak not sizzle, and they won't write a check for a "wow."
- *Profits.* Focus on generating profits by simultaneously lowering costs and increasing revenues.
- *Progress.* Infopreneurs progress when they provide better information to more people at lower costs.

# PART TWO

# BEYOND DATA AND DOLLARS

# 10

# INFLUENCE OF INFOPRENEURS

Now that we have analyzed how to succeed as an infopreneur, let us look beyond data and dollars to how infopreneurs are streamlining America's institutions and industries in this Information Revolution.

## STREAMLINING GOVERNMENT

Government institutions represent one of the most inflexible segments of American society. Interaction with new information technologies together with the realities of an information-saturated environment, makes it necessary for bureaucrats to reassess the structure of their respective organizations. The Information Age has forced public institutions to abandon unworkable policies and adopt new tactics. This is where the infopreneur comes in. Infopreneurs are helping to streamline the following institutions in response to the pressures of the Information Revolution:

- Congress
- National Archives
- Patent and Trademark Office
- CIA
- Census Bureau
- IRS
- Postal Service
- Public Education
- Peace Corps
- Pentagon
- Supreme Court

## Congress

The United States Congress is actually 535 separate information management businesses operating under one dome. Congressional representatives, as independent information handlers, are drowning in data:

- In 1964, 1649 journalists covered Congress. Twenty years later, 3748 reporters were assigned: seven journalists for every member of Congress.
- In 1972, Congress received 14.6 million pieces of computerized direct mail. Twelve years later, over 200 million pieces were received: 460,000 for each representative. On a single day, House Speaker Tip O'Neil received five million computer-generated letters.
- In 1984, 20,000 registered lobbyists, trade association officers, lawyers on retainer, and corporate liaison officials were paid to influence legislation: 37 lobbyists for every Congressional official.

- Thousands of details, ranging from hearings to floor votes, from handshakes to speeches, from campaigns to fund-raisers, have drawn the attention of Congress away from its main agenda: making laws.

Congress is a model of administrative inefficiency. Each day, hundreds of triple-carboned memos and regulatory rulings pass manually between offices. Infopreneurs in Congress are introducing interactive local area networks to improve office management, data gathering, accounting, word processing, and generation and dissemination of mail. These networks will also help legislators answer correspondence, monitor legislation, track media activities, and distribute memos among themselves.

Electronic information management is the best way for Congress to cope with its information overload. Once Congress becomes a better manager of its information, it can clearly focus on its more pressing agenda items.

## National Archives

The National Archives houses more than 1.25 billion square feet of paper. To make this information more manageable and accessible, infopreneurs are converting America's national memories into trillions of bits of optically stored graphic information. This is being accomplished through electronic scanning and transmission of data, image compression and display, and laser printing.

Infopreneurs initially researched the use of microfilm to reduce National Archives paperwork, yet cracking, fading, and poor duplication eliminated it as an option. However, when optical storage was introduced and found to provide durable and accurate duplication, 't was adopted as the conversion tool.

The first phase in converting the Archives' information consisted of electronic scanning, whereby nearly six billion images were captured, stored, and retrieved. The next phase of the program will integrate artificial intelligence systems to complete the conversion.

Computerized Archives information will allow all remote users to access information more efficiently. Software that allows cross-referencing also improves research capabilities.

The federal government is considering launching its own data satellite to provide electronic access to Archives material. Local data centers would act as clearinghouses, process information requests, and distribute data electronically. When completed, the conversion program will make access to information in the National Archives as easy as perusing a library card catalog.

## Patent and Trademark Office

The Patent and Trademark Office today struggles to fulfill its Constitutional mandate. The volume of patent and trademark applications, storage requirements, and retrieval requests has crippled the system. Over the years, the sheer bulk of 25 million patents and trademarks currently on file has resulted in two million of these documents being misplaced or lost. A two-year delay in processing 232,000 patent requests finally forced the office to set three objectives:

- Reduce the waiting period for a patent by 25 percent, from 24 months to 18 months.
- Decrease the processing time for trademarks.
- Fully automate all patent application and filing procedures by 1990.

These objectives will be accomplished as infopreneurs at the Patent and Trademark Office complete its computerization conversion.

Under the new system, applicants submit information to the office in any form, including computer disk. The information will then be converted by an optical character reader. Copies of computer files will be maintained on magnetic tape or hard disk. Examiners will access the computer file at work station terminals. Drawings will be reproduced from computer files through a process called automated photocomposition.

Documents that arrive at the Patent Office now receive bar codes similar to those used in grocery stores. New documents make up a data base known as LEXPAT, that permits instant access to patent or trademarks at any time. By 1990, about 500,000 patents will be part of this data base.

## CIA

The Central Intelligence Agency is America's spy service. Headquartered in Langley, Virginia, the CIA employs approximately 18,000 information handlers who gather information which enhances its espionage capabilities to deter Soviet theft of American technology, to uncover the $80 billion a year drug traffic industry, to eliminate international terrorism, and much more.

Infopreneurs of the CIA's intelligence analysis piece together information to improve the government's decision-making capabilities. At the heart of this intelligence analysis are the National Intelligence Estimates (NIEs), which predict world events ranging from Soviet weaponry to Third World terrorism.

The Reagan Administration, which depends heavily on the information provided by the CIA, upgraded its capabilities by increasing the CIA's budget to nearly two billion dollars a year. This financial impetus allows the CIA to process more information faster. In 1980, for example, only 12 NIEs were created; three years later, the CIA produced 50.

Looking further ahead than most other government agencies, the CIA uses its information to provide early warnings of future problems. A major government reorganization under consideration would make the National Security Advisor coordinator of all U.S. intelligence operations. This move exemplifies the importance of consolidating the CIA's information to help America define its priorities into the twenty-first century.

### Census Bureau

In planning for the 1990 census, statistical experts and infopreneurs are studying the feasibility of "dialing for demographics." The Census Bureau will save time and effort by using the telephone and the computer to count people instead of conducting home visits and mailing forms to residents. One procedure under consideration does not even require a respondent to own a phone—only to have access to one. This scenario involves automatic answering machines, modems, push button telephones, prerecorded messages, and computer-controlled dialogues. The respondent's census information would be directly entered into the Census Bureau's central computer via the respondent's push button phone.

Accurate Census Bureau information can also help reduce government waste and fraud. An example of such waste was uncovered by an audit of Health and Human Services which showed that more than $40 million in Social Security payments was sent to 8518 people listed as deceased in Medicare's records.

Now more than ever, computerized information from the Census Bureau is vital to the Inspectors General program to reduce government waste and fraud. As government spending exceeds $2 billion a day ($25,000 a second), the Inspectors General now audit the Departments of Agriculture, Commerce, Defense, Energy, Health and Human Services, Housing and Urban Development, Interior, Labor, State, Transportation, and Treasury, as well as Community Services, General Services, National Aeronautics and Space Administration, Small Business and Veterans Administrations, Environmental Protection Agency, and Agency for Internal Development. In six months under this audit program, the Inspectors General realized $5.8 billion in direct savings and improved use of funds.

The technological solution to the problem of government waste within the Census Bureau is the conversion of all manual audit systems into a single computerized system. This system can be programmed to automatically cross-check among other departments to isolate errors, abuse, fraud, and waste.

The Census Bureau should also tap into the IRS data base to obtain demographic data between decades. After all, Americans report more about themselves, financially speaking, every year to to the IRS than they do every ten years to the Census Bureau.

## IRS

On July 1, 1862, the Office of the Commissioner of Internal Revenue was established. It levied the first individual income tax to help pay for the Civil War. Fifty years later, the sixteenth Amendment paved the way for a federal individual income tax. With more than 600 million pieces of paper constituting tax returns filed in 1984, and with storage costs alone exceeding $10 million per year, the National Computer Center for the IRS pleaded for a more efficient and accurate system. In 1985, Congress enforced the disk-filing law which requires companies with more than 50 returns to submit them to the IRS on magnetic disk or tape. This is only one part of an extensive program to redesign the Internal Revenue Service.

Infopreneurs at the IRS are in the initial phase of the Tax Redesign Project which, by the year 2006, will have overhauled the country's entire tax collection system. IRS agents will pull floppy disks from files, place them into personal computers, then file income tax returns electronically. Evaluations and refunds will be issued instantly. The project will eliminate the bulk of the IRS paper-handling and storage costs through state-of-the-art hardware and software, increase IRS efficiency, lower its long-term costs, while producing a quick payback on this multibillion-dollar outlay.

## Postal Service

Established in 1775, the Post Office was one of America's first information management organizations. More than two centuries later, the Post Office is in crisis. In 1985, the U.S. Postal Service delivered 604 letters for every U.S. citizen and ran up a deficit of $750 million caused by:

- *Deregulation.* The airlines dropped unprofitable routes leading the Postal Service to spend $150 million to cover the routes.
- *Increased mail volume.* The Post Office will deliver 192 billion pieces of mail in 1990—an increase of 6.5 percent each year.

- *Unplanned labor increase.* More than 40,000 new employees were hired to maintain the current service level with the increased mail volume. Today labor costs absorb 83 cents of every postal dollar.

To boost efficiency, infopreneurs at the Postal Service integrated more than $500 million of new information technology: automated mail-sorting machines to improve sorting efficiency, computer terminals at local post offices to speed up window service, and electronic scales and microcomputers to replace rate books and information manuals.

Today's infopreneurs continue to chip away at the Postal Service's monopoly as MCI's Bill McGowan did with AT&T's telephone monopoly. Since 1976, private firms have delivered the mail in some 5000 rural routes. More than 70 percent of all parcels are now handled by United Parcel Service, a private mail delivery company. More than 40 percent of the multibillion-dollar overnight priority mail market is controlled by Federal Express.

Information Age businesses have chosen to bypass the Postal Service by using electronic document transmission and retrieval. Corporate decision makers refuse to wait three days for the Post Office's computer-sorted, jet-transported, highway-driven letter when they can send the same letter electronically in a matter of minutes. As this trend continues, the Post Office may be the next monopoly dismantled.

## Public Education

Because the number of supercomputers is increasing at a rate of 60 percent a year, there is a concern that the United States will not have enough skilled engineers to manage them. Universities are playing a key role in training computer technicians to meet the needs created by new technology.

As technology changes the way business is conducted, infopreneurs within universities are responding by teaching the skills future business leaders will need to compete in a world economy. Universities have begun to tailor their curricula to the corporation of the future.

A survey of leading graduate business schools shows that more than 50 percent already created custom education programs for corporations. In addition, both large and small universities are stressing the need for familiarity with computers through their curricula. One-third of the 12 million students currently enrolled in college own a computer.

The business/university relationship will require guidelines as it continues to develop. Businesses should only recommend subject areas to schools rather than specify curricula so that schools will not be forced to compromise their educational control. Together, universities and businesses can tailor programs to the needs of the student and the corporation.

Universities have not entered the Information Age without expense. Progressive universities have designed state-of-the-art networks that connect computers throughout their campuses. Some universities have invested up to $50 million in their computer centers to improve academic research and enhance their curricula. Although the millions of dollars spent do not provide a guarantee against obsolescence, the cost to society of not having the trained infopreneurs will be much higher.

## Peace Corps

At least 800 million people in Third World countries exist on a diet so limited that they cannot carry on routine activities. Each day, more than 40,000 people die of malnutrition and infection. In response to this worldwide problem, the Kennedy Administration created the Peace Corps to promote Third World self-sufficiency. After 25 years, the Peace Corps is in transition. The impact of information technology and the reduced cost of international data transmission have transformed the organization. It may soon become an *electronic Peace Corps*.

The major benefit of an electronic Peace Corps is that messages can be sent anywhere in a matter of seconds. Through the use of packet-switching equipment, infopreneurs in developing countries can tap data bases for vital information from around the world. The cost of such data transmission is as low as $1.00 per 1000 words—actually cheaper than the cost of mailing a local letter within the United States.

The applications for such a program are unlimited:

- Physicians can check their diagnoses against data bases for the proper prescriptions.
- Health care organizations can study and effectively treat epidemics.
- Nations can establish efficient food distribution systems for peoples struck by famine.

The use of the computer to share information has changed the world. A Third World country can link its computer to data bases in America to solve its internal problems. Slow and inflexible government agencies in developing countries are bypassed as infopreneurs obtain vital information to improve the quality of life.

## Pentagon

Strategies for World War III have been designed by military experts with the assistance of infopreneurs. The Pentagon's 8000 computers secure America's defense as military software gathers, stores, and analyzes both overt and covert information to simulate battle scenarios.

Military strategists and information professionals have worked together for more than a decade to develop battlefield training aids that provide field officers with instant answers to fast-changing combat scenarios. Pentagon computers create detailed images of any battlefield on earth. These "video battlefields" portray buildings, roads, rivers, even weapon systems. Battles are programmed to occur at the same pace as in actual combat.

Technological research and development has been an essential component of U.S. military strategy since the mobilization of scientists during World War II. United States military technology, which accounts for more than ten percent of military spending, resulted in the creation of a complex military information network. Early warning satellites orbiting 22,000 miles above the equator detect enemy missiles and send warnings to communications satellites. These warnings are passed on to the North American Aerospace Defense Command (NORAD) in Colorado, which communicates with the Strategic Air Command, the White House, the Pentagon, and numerous mobile radio vans. Mobile and fixed networks provide a constant flow of information for the President and Joint Chiefs of Staff. Bomber fleets, ICBM bases, ballistic missile submarines, and airborne fleets can simultaneously communicate through various information networks.

The Pentagon has also tested advanced artificial intelligence applications for the battlefield. Robots now act as hands and sensors on hazardous and repetitive military projects.

Even with these communication and information breakthroughs, Pentagon computers are America's biggest security concern. Defense Department computers are vulnerable to numerous spy and sabotage tactics:

- *Trojan Horse*—allows an unauthorized user access to computers.
- *Spoof*—feigns normal activity as it collects specific top secret information.
- *Virus*—hides undetectable instructions deep within software to destroy or alter computer data.

The nature of war has remained constant throughout the centuries. Weapons, warheads, and the military's armed forces are only the means of war. War itself is a set of constraints that resists an enemy's impositions. Along with these constraints, America's battle and war scenarios are being designed by Pentagon strategists with the help of infopreneurs.

## Supreme Court

As the Information Revolution creates new roles for infopreneurs, corporations, and nations, new guidelines need to be defined regarding the rights and limits of information ownership. Supreme Court rulings on cases dealing with information in various forms, such as copyrights, trade secrets, investor tip sheets, libel, electronic bandits, the Freedom of Information Act, and espionage touch the very soul of the Information Revolution.

First Amendment interpretation by the Supreme Court in recent years has encouraged creative expression and full dissemination of information. But this deregulated environment presents a unique set of problems. For example, should the information in a computer conference be considered the same as information in a telephone conversation, that is, in the public domain or privately owned—and worthy of a copyright? Some participants in computer conferences now insert copyright notices in their "conversations." The Supreme Court enforces the Copyright Act of 1976 under which electronic messages of conferences are implicitly copyrighted in the names of participants, whether or not a copyright notice is included. Yet, if the infopreneur does not obtain a copyright within five years, legal ownership of the conversation is forfeited.

A recent court case highlights the complexities of off-the-air recordings. Universal Studios is suing Sony Corporation to stop it from selling videotape machines. Universal hopes to eliminate the home taping of its copyrighted audio-visual materials. A panel of federal judges at one point concluded that the recording of materials on videotape recorders for private, noncommercial use does infringe on Universal Studios' copyrighted materials. The Supreme Court may have the final say on this issue.

The Supreme Court now has the power to shape the Information Revolution. Its court rulings will have a profound impact on the life and well-being of both individuals and corporations as the scope of information usage is broadened or restricted. All of this must be interpreted on the basis of past Congressional legislation and court rulings. Supreme Court rulings will affect electronic bulletin boards, VCRs, satellite transmission, computer data bases, and photocopying of books and articles. Such technologies and applications could never have been imagined by the writers of the First Amendment.

## Government's Paper Mountain

The Information Revolution, sparked by technological advances, forced government institutions to call in the infopreneurs. The result has been the streamlining of the institutions to better manage the influx of information to be processed and stored. However the accessibility of low-cost personal computers, desktop printers, and photocopy machines has actually increased, rather than decreased, the amount of paper used.

Between 1981 and 1985, the volume of paper documents increased from 850 billion to 1.4 trillion pages. This is a paradox in light of the optical disk's memory capacity: one side stores up to 54,000 pages of information, the equivalent of a complete set of encyclopedias.

The Information Revolution has not eliminated paper's role, but in fact, redefined it. In the Agrarian Age, paper was primarily used to store information. With introduction of the movable press in the fifteenth century, paper became a way to easily transfer information. In the twentieth century, the introduction of computerized word and data processing again changed the role of paper to that of managing information.

The challenge that faces infopreneurs in government is not so much how to eliminate paper, but how to increase paper's potential for stimulating decision-oriented action.

Computers have reduced both the time and the paper involved in document preparation. But the belief that computerization will lead to a paperless government is as preposterous as the belief that Gutenberg's movable press would eliminate books.

# STREAMLINING BUSINESS

Since the 1973 oil embargo, business owners and managers have been hiring infopreneurs to help streamline their businesses to cope with the new economic realities of the Information Age:

- *Saturation in the demand for goods.* By 1970, 99 percent of American households had radios, television sets, and refrigerators.
- *Costs of mass-produced goods.* With costs for labor and energy rising, the subsequent cost to manufacture goods of equal quality increased.
- *Competition from other goods producers.* Third World producers with cheap energy and low labor costs can export better and cheaper products than can be produced in America.

By 1999, information processing and delivery will account for half of all service sector jobs. Because of this shift in the economy, information is now considered a strategic business weapon. Companies use information to support their basic businesses and differentiate themselves from the competition. Information management systems help companies become strategically positioned in the new information environment.

The information industry, a $525 billion segment of the world's economy, actually encompasses all businesses that produce information, offer it as a service, or provide the means of handling it. Embedded processing, perhaps the best way for American manufacturers to compete with overseas production, occurs when information technology is packaged into products to make them smarter, longer lasting, easier to repair, and less consumptive of energy.

As business turns to information to streamline itself, infopreneurs and their information economy will supplement, rather than supplant the industrial economy. The combination of data processing and communications will increase industrial productivity just as industry contributed to the increased productivity within agriculture.

The information economy now substitutes information-intensive capital for energy-intensive capital. It is this dynamic that represents the cornerstone of future productivity gains. For example, telecommunications and information management capabilities help conserve resources. Reducing American business travel (airlines and automobiles) by only one percent over the last decade would have saved about 25 million barrels of oil.

However, information technology seems to be the enemy of corporate bureaucrats. An infopreneur's ability to design, arrange, and manage complex information tasks makes many middle-level management jobs unnecessary. It is not the young, educated, risk-taking managers that resist the new technologies. Rather it is the aging executives and managers entrenched in the large, old-line companies having the greatest trouble integrating the new technology to streamline their operations.

As the information marketplace grows, information buyers become more demanding and discriminating about the information they purchase. They seek information that helps them find competitive advantages in the following areas:

- Prospecting and sales.
- Travel and entertainment.
- Operations management.
- Purchasing and distribution.
- Promotion and advertising.
- Customer service.
- Information management.
- Manufacturing.
- Personnel and training.
- Retailing.

The challenge to infopreneurs throughout the Information Revolution will be to help businesses quantify the return on investment from their information and information system purchases relative to the value of better and faster information handling.

## Prospecting and Sales

Infopreneurs have introduced computer programs to optimize prospecting and selling. With the average salesperson receiving $42,000 in training prior to earning his or her first dollar for the company, computerized telemarketing has helped these salespersons reach more customers more often for far less money than through conventional sales avenues.

In addition to the average cost of an industrialized sales call surpassing $240, it takes an average of 5.5 sales visits to close a sale. With telephone marketing software packages, the salesperson can stay organized by not only programming who to call next, but even let the computer dial the phone numbers itself. One-key commands can produce labels, letters, order forms, envelopes, lists of customers, prospects, special products, prices, inventory, and more. With the current cost of the average business-to-business outbound telephone call at $5.00, and the standard business letter at $7.00, the sales cost through electronic correspondence drops significantly.

When one salesman goes on the road, he takes a laptop computer with him to search for other prospects within the regions he is visiting. By punching in the regional zip codes, the computer goes through its list of current prospects and recommends those whom he should visit. At the end of the week, the computer can print out who was visited, how many phone calls were made, how much time was spent on the phone, and how many letters were sent. The computer then compares the effectiveness of each selling method, as well as the effectiveness of calls made at different times of the day and different days of the week.

Infopreneurs have also introduced flexible and convenient ways to boost sales through electronic marketing systems such as "in-store" systems, electronic point-of-sale systems, and "public-access" systems.

In-store systems, such as Buick's EPIC, use interactive videodisk technology to demonstrate products that cannot be easily handled or displayed in the store. They assist shoppers in selecting products and completing purchases. Buick qualified 4000 potential customers at an auto show in New York, then passed the leads on to its telemarketing department and dealers.

Electronic point-of-sale machines (EPOS), which are similar to a bank's automated teller machines, provide access to services such as airline ticket purchases or hotel reservations.

Public-access systems use computer-generated text and illustrations to display travel, recreation, entertainment, shopping, and other information of interest. These systems are often seen in public locations such as malls, convention centers, and airports.

Infopreneurs have also introduced computer-aided sales forecasting. For a product division manager with a 70- or 7000-item product line that needs updating each month for material requirements planning, the computer is the best aid available. When a company redraws sales territory to improve distribution, computer forecasting can help plan the best places to advertise, which trade shows to attend, and what the overall budget should be. With proper programming, the computer takes into account all the relevant variables affecting a product or product line, and produces a sum effect, at the punch of a few buttons.

## Travel and Entertainment

Corporations closely monitor not only their actual sales figures but also the cost to make the sales. One of the factors most heavily weighed into this figure is the salesperson's travel and entertainment expenses, affectionately known in the industry as the T&E. IBM, for example, spends over $500 million a year to move its 395,000 executives, managers, and lower-level personnel around the country to attend meetings and visit customers.

Even though this figure amounts to about 1 percent of its total revenue, IBM is aggressively campaigning to pare its costs for business travel. By introducing a travel management system, IBM is depending on its highly computerized system to manage the complex business of travel. Business and industry should learn some valuable lessons as infopreneurs within IBM consolidate the services of 2000 travel agents into a travel management system.

Teleconferencing breakthroughs have also helped to reduce T&E expenses. American Video Teleconferencing has introduced a system that transmits live data, still pictures, and voice by phone for only $60 per hour for an average of four hours a day among corporate offices. This is quite competitive when compared to the $1000 per hour cost for renting a video teleconferencing room which often only transmits voices and picture, yet no data. The judicial system is also turning to telephone conferencing in lieu of court appearances to unclog the courts and trim attorney's fees.

## Operations Management

Infopreneurs leverage the new computer architecture and software to create "smart machines" which not only tell how they arrive at solutions, but carry on dialogues and print out the rules they use to arrive at their solutions. This technology results in better systems maintenance, quicker debugging, and the achievement of goals in shorter time frames. For example, as a management aid, smart systems help weigh the pros and cons of critical decisions. Relevant data for each alternative are entered and the computer generates its recommendations.

Smart systems can monitor the business performance of various departments and actually interact with personnel. If, for instance, sales, costs, or inventories get out of line, a memo can be automatically generated to the department head requesting both an explanation of the situation and corporate action necessary to remedy the problems.

Data security is one of the most volatile issues in operations management today. Infopreneurs have introduced passwords, personal identification, and data encryption to control access to classified information. New methods have recently been introduced which record characteristics such as fingerprints, blood-vessel patterns in the retina of the eye, length of the fingers, lines that crisscross the palm, or voice waves. When such characteristics match those in the computer's memory, access to the computer is granted.

Smart systems can even monitor a "user style" of the current operator. Should the user style change or vary significantly, the computer will assume it is being tampered with and close down.

Infopreneurs are even introducing services which can help

an existing company go national overnight. Headquarters Companies—HQ—is a nationwide network of fully operational office space and service centers located throughout the United States. Every HQ Center comes with a complete support staff supervised by a professional management team, which includes full secretarial and mail service, telephone answering, word processing, conference room facilities, telex, facsimile, teleconferencing, phone-in dictation, 800 number service, on-premise travel ticketing, and of course, private offices.

HQ Centers take care of every facet of office administration, from staffing to equipment maintenance. The expanding company's identity goes on the building directory, in the phone listing, even on the doors to the offices. The only thing missing are the administrative hassles and the expense of a conventional office.

## Purchasing and Distribution

Computerized distribution created the "overnight industry." Federal Express is a three-billion-dollar-a-year overnight package airfreight service that delivers an average of 300,000 packages each day. Perhaps no other company in business today is as dependent on computers as Federal Express. With around-the-clock monitoring as part of its service, each package is assigned a bar code serial number. A scanner with an internal clock display and keyboard monitors each of the six times a package changes hands in the overnight delivery schedule. This information system gives Federal Express absolute control—one reason they lead the overnight industry in volume and efficiency.

Computerized ordertaking has become a way for companies to control distribution and inventory costs. At two Hewlett-Packard plants where measurement instruments are manufactured, daily deliveries of the flat aluminum sheet from suppliers are essential to eliminate storage costs and minimize production costs. The metals service center computerized its manufacturing site to coordinate its warehousing and shipping with H-P's needs.

An effective purchasing and distribution management system often includes electronic invoicing where data linkage between the purchaser and the supplier replaces written invoices. For some firms that want to ease into electronic invoicing, weekly telexes are already replacing billing by mail. Today, most invoices are produced by computer at the vendor, printed on paper, and reentered into a different computer by the customer. Electronic invoicing reduces the time required to move data from a vendor to a customer from eight days down to one.

Consumers have been purchasing electronically for years. With more than 6500 different mail order catalogues published every year, the growth of this $50 billion dollar a year industry is attributed to the convenient application of tele-mail—ordering by phone and receiving goods by mail.

Pitney Bowes has even turned to the phone for the purchasing and distribution of postage. For customers to refill their postage meters by phone, they simply make a toll-free call and their RMRS postage meter is refilled within 90 seconds. For the customer this postage by phone system means no more trips to the post office or running out of postage in the middle of a mailing.

One reason companies have turned to infopreneurs to help automate their purchasing and distribution is for cost reductions. For example, Johnson & Johnson Hospital Services launched COACT On-Line Procurement System to consolidate customer service and distribution for J&J's 15 medical equipment, supply, and pharmaceutical companies. The system saves customers from 2 to 8 percent of the costs of purchasing products. Other benefits besides cost reduction include creation of a national distribution network, on-line information access, consolidated customer reports, automated order entry, and improved productivity.

Infopreneurs within the Campbell Soup Company pointed out that information provides an advantage in purchasing and inventory control. Soon after, its management information staff was doubled and its operating budget tripled. Hand-held computers now scan labels of shelf products, record the order quantity and delivery requirements, and forward the information to regional computers via communications modem, any hour of the day or night. The information system sends error-less orders to its computers, eliminating the burden of written reports.

## Promotion and Advertising

Infopreneurs have transformed Geico Insurance Company's marketing effort by inviting drivers to compare insurance rates in ten minutes over the phone, 24 hours a day. Geico's direct marketing program, "The 10-Minute Surprise" asks, "Is saving $70 on your car insurance worth a 10-minute phone call?" Geico operators are accessible around-the-clock, 365 days a year to compare costs for callers. By eliminating the overhead associated with satellite offices, insuring safe drivers, and conducting business directly by phone, Geico *claims* to provide a better service at lower prices.

One infopreneur started American Discount Stamps which sells first-class postage for more than 20 percent off the first-class rate. Profits accrue from advertising revenues. With a regulation postage stamp already affixed to the upper right hand corner of a two-by-three inch advertising sticker, the advertising revenue more than offsets the nickel lost in postage fees for each sticker. Discount stamps represent the first new advertising medium to come along since television.

Computer $olution is a computerized device that prints out promotional coupons at the checkout counter after an item is scanned, and issues certain coupons based on the product bought. Coupons are handed to the customer by the checker at the end of the sale along with the register receipt. These coupons can stimulate purchases of new brands or similar products. For example, coupons for decaffeinated coffee can be generated for anyone who purchases caffeine-free soft drinks.

Harris Catalog Library is promoting mail order catalogs by placing catalog kiosks in public libraries. The nonelectronic kiosks attractively display more than 500 catalogs for browsing. The kiosk has complete and easy instructions for ordering either with catalog coupons or with standard order forms supplied by HCL.

Proctor & Gamble has turned to electronic marketing to help defend its territory in the annual $950 million toothpaste market. P&G randomly telephones people; if they respond that Crest is the dentist's choice to keep teeth tartar-free, they receive $25. The telephone quiz represents a break from traditional advertising markets.

## Customer Service

In the Information Age, customer service may be a company's most potent marketing weapon. Companies like American Express, GE, Sony, IBM, and others have realized the importance of customer service and invested hundreds of millions of dollars into computers, data banks, communications lines, personnel, and training to make their conglomerates assume the flavor of large mom-and-pop drugstores.

Service not only ties customers more closely into their corporations, but the close interaction with customers provides them with significant market information. Infopreneurs can sort through the market input to generate demographic data, evaluate advertising impact, identify problems with merchandise, provide clues to customer concerns, assess product life-expectancies, determine the competence of customers for repairing products from home, and isolate new ideas for products and services.

Even more impressive are the changing attitudes toward customer problems. Companies are actually soliciting complaints from customers and tying these buyers' perceived views into the design, manufacturing, and sale of products and services. To become more accessible to their customers, companies now advertise their toll-free numbers. For example, *Time* magazine places its Customer Service Renewal Hotline on the same page as letters to the editor. Easy instructions guarantee uninterrupted delivery of *Time* through the convenience of its hotline.

Everything from travel reservations and financial services to goods and advice can now be obtained by calling any of the

400,000 toll-free numbers offered in the marketplace. More than four billion toll-free calls were placed last year.

Perhaps the most significant trend in customer service is the talking computer. Voice response, the technology that enables computers to communicate through speech, is starting to catch on. Voice response can minimize the need for human operators and reduce human error in data entry transactions by up to 50 percent.

The Touch Tone capabilities have turned the telephone into a computer terminal that taps into computer data bases or sends information via phone lines. Computerized voice response systems can deliver correct prices complete with customer-specific discounts. The information is calculated by the computer and immediately fed back over the telephone—in words. As part of an integrated computer voice response system, invoices and shipping records can be printed and ready to mail within minutes of satisfying the customer's need.

At a liquor distribution center voice response technology handles phone orders over 16 telephone lines. The director of the center's management information system estimates that voice response saves the company an amount equivalent to the wages of 11 employees.

One pharmacy uses the computer-generated voice technology to help improve patient compliance while simultaneously ensuring repeat business and customer loyalty. The process of filling a prescription starts with a computer that notifies the voice response unit when to place a call to the patient. At the proper time, the information from the patient profile becomes part of the computer script. The patient is told by the computer that if medication has been taken according to the physician's instructions, it is due for a refill.

Since patients do not feel threatened by the computer voice, they tend to respond well. Patients can push their phone key pads to indicate that they will reorder and come in to pick up the refill. The system flags any prescriptions that have not been picked up or refilled for follow-up by the pharmacist.

Customer service is now depending on infopreneurs and their technology to solve problems while reducing costs. The

Touch Tone telephone has become an automatic link with a customer service data base which lets customers respond in a warm, friendly, human voice, not the harsh sound of a computer, 24 hours a day, 365 days a year for as little as 25 cents an hour.

## Information Management

In 1983, a high school junior read about a credit card that used laser technology to store up to 800 pages of data. This perceptive infopreneur concluded that if the card could work in conjunction with the personal computer, it would have significant impact on business.

Even though more than 5000 companies had inquired about the potential applications of the laser card from its inventor, they all waited for someone else to lead the way. So this young infopreneur presented the card to Blue Cross-Blue Shield of Maryland as a way to centralize patient files and as an identification system to tell which of its 1.6 million subscribers are entitled to which benefits. The patient card is placed into a computer slot, its contents read on the screen, and comments typed directly onto the card itself. Patients can actually carry their entire medical files in their wallets.

At age 20, this infopreneur became a senior information management consultant to Blue Cross on its $48 million contract, receives a six-figure consulting fee, and part ownership in the venture, as well as royalties from each software system sold.

Information management was also behind the 1985 Live-Aid concert viewed by more than two billion people worldwide. Pulled together in only ten weeks, the 17-hour concert featured 60 acts split between Philadelphia and London. The performances were beamed live via 13 satellites to more than 110 countries. More than $60 million were pledged by program's end through a toll-free phone number.

Even sports fanatics can leverage information storage and management services. Computer Sports World is a computerized data base with more than 4500 files of up-to-the-minute sports information. Sports junkies have information at their fingertips on demand. By calling Computer Sports World, infopreneurs provide callers with the latest scores, match ups, injuries, statistics, weather, odds, and racing results from more than 60 thoroughbred tracks. Computer Sports World takes payment from all major credit cards.

## Manufacturing

The Information Revolution has ushered in dramatic changes in consumer products and the ways they are manufactured. Many products now process information as part of their normal functioning. A dishwasher's control system directs various components of the unit through the washing cycle and visually displays the process to the owner.

In the automobile industry, infopreneurs have had a significant influence in the manufacturing of cars. Traditionally, when a company wanted to test a car in a wind tunnel, it had to build a wind tunnel. Computers can now simulate a car in a computer-simulated wind tunnel. This pure informational process improves a car's design, performance, and reliability. As a safety feature, some automobiles are even equipped with "drowsiness-warning systems" that recognize when the car comes too close to other cars, curbs, or obstacles. A new product, Titan Auto Kill is activated by telephone when the car owner realizes that a theft has occurred. The call triggers a siren and continually flashes the car's lights. When the thief pulls over and opens the door to stop the alarm, the engine shuts down and cannot be restarted.

Mass production, which involves standardized, single-purpose machines, breaks down every task into simple steps carried out by semiskilled labor. The manufacturing sector's special purpose machines, centralized capital and human resources, rigid work roles, and supplier domination by mass producers have become less productive in the Information Revolution.

The shift into the Information Age introduced a breakthrough in computer-based production which uses skilled laborers with general-purpose machinery to produce a wide assortment of goods for constantly shifting markets.

Computer-integrated manufacturing (CIM) is the next step toward the paperless factory. CIM centralizes all the information necessary from engineering to design to manufacturing. In the 1950s when the environment was less competitive, it was of little consequence if a product from concept to distribution took up to a decade. But with today's heightened competition, computer-integrated manufacturing can reduce production schedules from years to a matter of just months.

Finally, made-to-measure suits can now be ordered and delivered at half the traditional price in less than a week. Custom Vetement Associates mass produces custom-ordered clothing for American retailers through a French garment factory. Rather than repeated fittings and hand-cut cloth, computers, lasers, and satellite communications create significant savings in both cost and time.

After the salesperson takes the customer's measurements, the data is entered into a computer. A telephone WATS line links the U.S. retailer via satellite with the French manufacturer. A computer selects the correct fabric and the laser beam cuts the cloth to the customer's preference. The order and cloth-cutting process is complete in less than five minutes. The garment is then sewn by tailors with operational hand-stitched details. In four days the suit is ready and on its way to the retailer. The "computerized suit," depending on style, fabric, and retailer mark-up, can cost as little as $325 while its custom suit counterpart traditionally costs upwards of $750.

## Personnel and Training

Job-hunting can now be accomplished by computer or Touch Tone phone. Some employers now accept résumés on-line. The Maryland Job Board lets people dial a phone number, tap in a seven-digit identification code of the job category desired, and furnishes the caller a list of openings. The heart of this telephone service is the voice-mail technology.

Once an applicant is called in for an interview, he or she may take a 45-minute honesty test, which is 85 percent as accurate as a polygraph test. The tests can weed out potentially dishonest employees. Consisting of 90 honesty/dishonesty questions, plus six pages of fill-in questions on background, drug use, and criminal records, the test costs about $10 per person.

As for training, three infopreneurs have taken the $1.6 billion corporate seminar industry by the tail. They now make accessible desired programs for shoppers with just a phone call. The 1st Seminar Service of Lowell, Massachusetts, has enrolled hundreds of seminar suppliers who pay a 20 to 30 percent commission per enrollment. Its computerized data base can manage up to 60,000 seminars simultaneously. A client calls a toll-free number, states the type of seminar desired, time, and locations. At no cost to the client, the appropriate literature is forwarded, and, if needed, a space booked for the seminar.

Infopreneurs and their technology have also influenced training in the marketplace. Flight simulators represent a significant breakthrough, as they can simulate for airline pilots engine fires, weather hazards, traffic, control failures, and wheel-up landings. Without pilots ever leaving the ground, airlines save millions of dollars a year training pilots on the newest models of flight simulators which store up to 20,000 rules and can retrieve 100 million data items.

Perhaps the most volatile issue throughout the end of the century will be AIDS in the workplace. Infopreneurs with the *Personnel Journal* have developed a data base of reference materials about this modern day plague. The data base includes names of companies that have AIDS policies, bibliographies of articles on AIDS in the workplace, names of consultants, lawyers and other professionals who deal with AIDS issues.

## Retailing

Infopreneurs have also revolutionized America's retailing industry:

In 1976, the Price Club opened its doors for business and launched the $4 billion off-priced retail industry. From an abandoned airplane hangar, the Price Club offered brand-name, top-quality merchandise at an average mark-up of 9.5

percent. This figure is phenomenal in comparison to industry averages of 50 percent at department stores, 30 percent at discount stores, and 20 percent at food retailers. Each store has a computerized information management system that controls the inventory in an environment that generates sales of $600 per square foot—ten times the volume of discount retailers. Each Price Club outlet averages $108 million in annual sales and turns over its inventory up to 18 times a year—three times more than the average discount store.

Infopreneurs designed the information system which lets the Price Club buy directly from manufacturers, thereby eliminating wholesale middlemen. Since vendors allow 30 days for payment and the Price Club turns over its inventory within the month, it actually operates with no net investment. This translates into 100 percent vendor financing.

The Scottish and Irish Import Shop also utilizes the information insights of infopreneurs to sell its products. A product catalog and toll-free number expanded its local and tourist trade into a national business with revenues that surpass in-store receipts. Each of the seven years the catalog has been in existence, the business expanded at a 100 percent growth rate. Giving the customer a toll-free phone number provides a no-risk excuse to call.

The average order of $50 costs just $1.90 to process by phone and credit card. The information technology has given the Scottish and Irish Import Shop the flexibility to locate its catalog division to another county and tap into a more cost-efficient labor pool.

The L.L. Bean company keeps its Freeport, Maine location open 24 hours a day, 365 days a year for those who shop in person. For those who wish to shop by catalog, Bean has designed a direct response marketing program to service three million customers worldwide—around the clock, of course. L.L. Bean's computerized tracking system helps maintain control over its 30,000 orders placed each day through 200 operators sitting in front of IBM terminals. When a customer calls to place an order, the operator knows whether the item is in stock, when and how it can be delivered.

J.C. Penney has introduced Telaction, an interactive cable-subscribed "shopping mall." The service is hailed as being the first "consumer-controlled" home shopping service. Telaction uses a Touch Tone phone and dedicated cable TV to display a selection of stores and merchandise reminiscent of a mall. After dialing an 800 number to get into the system, a special number accesses entrance to shopping and buying. Store or major credit cards or personal checks are used to make the purchases.

Television shopping shows have actually spawned a new breed of retailer. Home shopping clubs and telephone auctions are now broadcast around the clock, sometimes on independent and cable channels. The developers of television shopping shows have worked with infopreneurs to combine two very popular American pastimes: shopping and watching television. They now move millions of dollars of merchandise each week. Though still in its infancy, retailing's newest breakthrough is receiving rave reviews.

## Concluding Thought

Change is always new, but the process of change is not. The Industrial Revolution was sparked by the application of new technology and new ideas which changed the role and function of human labor. The Information Revolution is again the application of new technology and new ideas. But this revolution is being led by infopreneurs who are expanding the function of information to streamline business.

As infopreneurs change the role of information they are having a significant impact on business and industry:

- Of the 21 million jobs created since 1970, nearly 19 million have been formed within the service sector.
- In the middle of the 1981 and 1982 recession, the ratio of new business formations to business failures was 28 to 1 making these the strongest "new business" years ever, even though business failures reached a record high of 23,000.
- In 1983, 4 million new jobs were created—the largest single year jump in employment in American history, pushing

unemployment down to 9.2 percent from 10.8 percent one year earlier.

Besides job creation, one of the most significant influences on business by the infopreneur is the trend toward home-based work. The number of people working from home on a full-time or part-time basis has jumped 50 percent in the past decade. While the Internal Revenue Service reports by their tax returns that 13 million Americans work from home, AT&T estimates from phone bills this figure to be closer to 23 million.

Telecommunications experts also predict a sharp increase in the number of people who will work from home. More than 7.2 million jobs currently performed in the office soon may be conducted from home through the use of information and communication technology. Infopreneurs will make telecommuting commonplace as they work from home but communicate with their offices via computers, telephones, and couriers.

The basic influence of infopreneurs on business is a redefinition of the office. In the Information Age, your office is your actual location at the moment. Being "away from your desk" will mean being unplugged from your information and communications network.

# 11

# ON BECOMING AN INFOPRENEUR

As we come to the end of this book, I want to review how you can participate in the Information Revolution—perhaps the most important advice I have given. If you can come to grips with these issues as we complete our shift into the Information Age, you will succeed as an infopreneur.

In any revolution, fewer than 5 percent of those involved benefit directly and significantly from the rapid technological, political, or social upheaval. The infopreneurs who sparked the Information Revolution shared the following traits necessary to reap the benefits of the Information Age:

- Infopreneurs consider information the most critical resource in any successful venture.
- Infopreneurs realize that information is power only if they can obtain the right information in a timely manner.
- Infopreneurs are driven more by the psychological challenge than by personal income.
- Infopreneurs seize their opportunities from changes in demographics, needs, moods, perceptions, knowledge, or technology.
- Infopreneurs function within fundamental market values, thus finding a need and filling it. More often than not, they are first to provide a solution to a problem of the future.
- Infopreneurs develop ways to control the quality and quantity of information required to solve problems.
- Infopreneurs realize that every crisis is an opportunity in disguise. They use anomalies and aberrations to isolate early signs of change.
- Infopreneurs ask the right questions in the right order so that the appropriate decision is made as ineffective options and bad decisions are eliminated.

Infopreneurs sparked the Information Revolution by carving out in the information marketplace small niches which became the industry that is now changing the world.

To carve out a niche in the marketplace, infopreneurs start with ideas. When infopreneurs investigate better ways to accomplish a task, great ideas often erupt spontaneously from within their values structures. Once an idea takes root, it becomes a product or service which is then presented as a cause: showing the world a better way.

Infopreneurs who pioneer information industries tend to be strong individualists who exhibit above-average ambition when faced with new opportunities. Using their abilities to develop ideas, infopreneurs frequently bypass convention and policy to develop their innovative solutions. Their behavior is often direct and forceful, because they expect a great deal from themselves and fellow workers. Pioneering infopreneurs have strong organizational skills, which enables them to tackle significant challenges.

Formal education for the infopreneur is not a prerequisite to carving out a niche using information. The operating software for the majority of the microcomputer industry was developed by William Gates—a college dropout. Fred Smith's operations plan for an overnight mail service received a "C" on a term paper at Yale, yet Smith went on to launch a $4 billion a year industry with his overnight mail service—Federal Express.

Money is not a prerequisite for the infopreneur, either. Apple Computers, a Fortune 500 company, began in a garage with the money from the sale of Steve Jobs' Volkswagon and Steve Wozniak's calculators. Electronic Data Systems, the data processing company acquired by General Motors for $2.5 billion, was started by H. Ross Perot with only $1000.

What these infopreneurs possessed, above all, was an idea that made sense to them. Over time, the infopreneur freely manipulates an idea in a world of theory, testing its efficacy and creating a new reality. Criticism from unbelievers does not divert successful infopreneurs once they believe they are right, but only challenges them to hone their ideas to completeness. Ultimately, it is their uncompromising commitment to the idea that transforms it into a product or service. Thus, with time and hard work, the theory of the idea becomes a reality in the business world.

Infopreneurs who carve out new niches in business and industry always begin with ideas. The characteristics displayed by successful infopreneurs can be learned and integrated. Everyone has ideas, but some people are more prepared than others to take action on their ideas. To be an infopreneur, you must start with an attitude of expectancy toward great ideas coming your way. Such an attitude is reflected in statements as, "This is a great time to be alive," "I enjoy every minute I'm awake," or "The Information Revolution is one of the most exciting eras in history." How far you go with your ideas is in direct proportion to how far you expect to go.

Participating in the Information Revolution requires:

- A broad base of knowledge.
- Specialized skills in managing ideas.
- Hard work.

A broad base of knowledge means exposure to many subjects. Try first to develop a broad understanding of industries and trends, then hone your comprehension of specific applications and technologies. This strategy will help you link seemingly disparate ideas.

You must acquire specialized skills to manage your ideas. When most people encounter problems with an idea, they tend to discard it. Learn how to put ideas "on hold." You can then approach them from another angle at another time with a new perspective.

Once you are convinced of an idea's validity, be prepared to work hard. There is a strategy that makes hard work seem easy. First, create an environment that allows you to work with an idea. Then fashion your world to carry forth the idea. This will cultivate an enthusiasm that buffers your idea from negative criticism and produces the persistence necessary to stick with your idea. Remember, the world may not be ready to embrace your concept. Be prepared to work tenaciously through the lonely and discouraging times.

If you are not convinced that you have an idea with which you can participate in the Information Revolution, learn how to generate ideas. Important breakthroughs come not so much from big ideas, but from small ideas that build on each other. It is these small ideas which can produce a powerful synergism.

Instead of chasing the big idea, build from your small ones. You have several options. First, notice details. This is where most ideas emerge. When you detect subtle details in your environment, your reception toward new ideas heightens. Next, start to link your current ideas with old or discarded ones. When you combine ideas, new and better ones result. Another way to build from small ideas is to rearrange them. Place them in a new industry context or a different form. Finally, identify anomalies and aberrations in your environment. These often point to emerging opportunities.

Once you have developed your small ideas into a big idea, evaluate its validity. Determine whether the idea is worthy of your commitment by asking yourself the following questions:

- Is the idea currently being implemented?
- Does the idea solve a problem or meet a need?
- Does the idea have universal appeal?

If the idea *is* currently being implemented, then someone else has begun to carve that niche. However, a variation on the idea or a new market application may provide a new opportunity. If the idea does not solve a problem or meet a need, it will either fail or become short-lived. Finally, if the idea develops universal appeal, you may have the opportunity to create an entirely new information business and become a leader of the Information Revolution.

Evaluating the idea on a personal level is crucial. The idea may solve a problem or meet a need, and it may have universal appeal, but it might not fit you personally. If the idea does not coincide with your values, skill level, or interest, your subconscious mind will reject it in time.

If your idea passes the three-question validity test and is in harmony with your values, skills, and interests, put the idea on hold and gather more information. You will need to do some research to find out how and where to apply the idea. Gather market and industry data that will place your idea in one of the following categories:

- A new-to-the-world product or service.
- A new-line product or service.
- An addition to an existing product or service.
- An improvement or revision to a current or discarded product or service.
- A repositioning product or service.
- A cost-reducing product or service.

Once you have isolated your idea's role in the marketplace, you are ready to make an uncompromising commitment to the idea:

*Commit to never quit.*

To carve out a niche with information and become a leader in the Information Revolution, you need to start with an idea. To be successful with your idea, you need to:

- Expect big ideas to come your way.
- Develop a broad base of knowledge.
- Acquire specialized skills to work with your idea.
- Work hard.
- Build a big idea from small ones.
- Evaluate the validity of the idea.
- Determine whether the idea coincides with your values, skills, and interests.
- Find the idea's place in the market.
- Commit yourself to never quit.

Let me back up for a moment to bring some perspective to the revolution that is currently underway. American Revolutions occur about every 100 years. The first one took place in 1776 when British colonists in the New World protested the injustices of Parliament's claim to jurisdiction over them. The second revolution started after the Civil War when America's farm-based economy gave way to industrial pursuits. The third American Revolution has begun right on schedule. It is an economic and social restructuring that involves information and affects everyone who picks up a phone, uses a credit card, or logs into a computer. This Information Revolution began in a Northern California valley nestled between the Santa Cruz mountains and Mount Diablo.

In 1951, an industrial park was established in an undeveloped valley 50 miles south of San Francisco to generate revenue for Stanford University. Stanford leased the land to high-technology companies, and today more than 25,000 workers inhabit the 1530 square miles known as Silicon Valley.

The generic association of Silicon Valley was originated when infopreneur William Shockley's semiconductor laboratory switched from the traditional four-layer diodes to silicon for building its transistors. Silicon Valley soon became widely known as the center of the information industry.

Infopreneurs flocked to Silicon Valley because of its rich information network and state-of-the-art technology. But the information industry's greatest leap occurred 20 years after its inception, with the development of the microprocessor. In 1971, Ted Hoff developed the first microprocessor which served as the central processing unit to control computers. That tiny semiconductor chip paved the way for several information processing breakthroughs which included on-line data searches, satellite communications, telex, time sharing, videotex, and the personal computer. The microchip, about the same thickness and weight as a strand of hair, is at the center of the annual $525 billion worldwide information industry.

Of the many breakthroughs by infopreneurs during the Information Revolution, the most significant was the switch from analog to digital transmission of information.

Modern digital computers shuffle numbers and letters as groups of discrete ones and zeros, allowing for incomparable savings in time and energy consumption. Within a few years, virtually all information will become individual elements (ones and zeros) as analog-to-digital conversion becomes the standard. As the information industry penetrates international markets, this digitized world of communication has become the ammunition of the Information Revolution.

Infopreneurs are the revolutionaries in this third American Revolution. As change agents, infopreneurs advocate a new standard that promotes the greatest number of advantages along the least painful route of change.

When introducing change through normative (trend lines), coercive (immediate change), or empiricive (the education process) methods, the adversary that must be overcome in the marketplace is the perception that, "No doubt, your idea may be better, but at its worst, it may be worse than the status quo."

To overcome this adversary of change, infopreneurs must build rapport which reduces any real or imagined defensiveness. This starts by defining needs and wants of the participants. As infopreneurs present themselves as a solution to problems, they become positioned to turn data into dollars. It is the responsibility of each infopreneur to present accurate information which alleviates any fear of error and justifies the expenditures by businesses and government. To become effective change agents requires:

- Infopreneurs to take a personal stake in the Information Revolution and the global marketplace.

- Infopreneurs to be directly involved in the definition of and solution to society's problems.
- Infopreneurs to interface between the government and the private sector in the achievement of society's goals.
- Infopreneurs to develop means for establishing viable priorities for the Information Age.
- Infopreneurs to strive to improve the quality of life, provide a balance in the labor force, and increase society's productivity.

Six measurement criteria which will gauge the success of infopreneurs throughout the Information Revolution include:

1. *Profits*—As infopreneurs improve productivity in the marketplace.

2. *Jobs*—As infopreneurs rapidly expand employment.

3. *Income*—As infopreneurs accelerate the upward movement of wages and salaries.

4. *Stability*—As infopreneurs work through the private enterprise economy to keep inflation in check.

5. *Priorities*—As infopreneurs establish and pursue society's objectives.

6. *Expansion*—As infopreneurs participate in the global economy through instant communications.

In summary, the Information Revolution is changing the world. Every rule and role in society is being challenged. Personal fulfillment, economic security, career satisfaction and financial freedom cannot be considered "guaranteed rights."

The secret to making *your* mark in the Information Revolution and turning data into dollars is to develop a strategy that helps you easily adapt to changes during this transition into the Information Age. Finally, never forget the words of King Solomon from Ecclesiastes 12:13, "Fear God, and keep His commandments: for this is the whole duty of man."

# INDEX

# INDEX

# INDEX